Martin de Porres
A Saint for Our Time

MARTIN DE PORRES
A SAINT FOR OUR TIME

by Joan Monahan

Paulist Press
New York/Mahwah, N.J.

COVER ART AND INTERIOR ILLUSTRATIONS BY PATRICK KELLEY

COVER DESIGN BY LYNN ELSE

Library of Congress Cataloging-in-Publication Data

Monahan, Joan, 1926–
    Martin de Porres : a saint for our time / by Joan Monahan.
      p. cm.
    Includes bibliographical references.
    ISBN 0-8091-6700-X
    1. Martâin, de Porres, Saint, 1579–1639. 2. Christian saints—Peru—Biography.
I. Title.
BX4700 .M397 M66 2003
282'.092—dc21

2002006693

Published by Paulist Press
997 Macarthur Boulevard
Mahwah, New Jersey 07430

www.paulistpress.com

Printed and bound in the
United States of America

TABLE OF CONTENTS

*To the Dominican Sisters
of the Immaculate Heart of Mary
of Akron, Ohio*

Acknowledgments

Devotion to St. Martin has been fostered in this country particularly by the Southern Province of Dominican Friars who have Martin as their patron. Devotion to Martin was encouraged by the Dominican friars and sisters long before his canonization in 1962. The first shrine in his honor was opened in 1936 in Columbia, South Carolina. The shrine office was moved to Louisiana in 1997. In 2001, a permanent shrine was dedicated to Martin in Memphis, Tennessee. The Friars' "Vision Statement" reads in part: [Martin's] "prophetic spirit still leads people to Jesus Christ and to his reign of compassion and justice." I give my sincere thanks to the many Dominicans at the shrine and elsewhere who assisted me with this project.

Note to the Reader

Except for leaving off the accent on Martìn, I have chosen to use the Hispanic form of most names in an attempt to be truer to the time. Even that presents problems as "facts" become changed as they are handed down. For example, recent scholarship suggests that even Martin's last name, Porres, is a misspelling. His name may well have been Porras since that is the name recorded in the priory's book of professions when Martin took perpetual vows as a *hermano donado,* a donation or gift.

INTRODUCTION

This little book attempts to detail just a few of the recorded events of the life of St. Martin de Porres of Lima, Peru. The events related are derived for the most part from the stories told after Martin's death by those who knew him well. Shortly after his death, notarized depositions or testimonies were collected to advance the cause of his official canonization, as it was recognized from the very first that this extraordinary man was a saint.

Although holy, St. Martin's life at first glance may seem strange and hardly one to be imitated in this twenty-first century. Such is not the case, however, and Martin has much to teach us today. He is proposed as a model to lead us closer to Our Lord and Savior as we imitate in our own small ways the events of his life. In considering Martin as a model, it's important to remember that he lived almost 500 years ago in a time and place seemingly much different from our own. However, if we peel away the crust of ages, we will find many similarities. First, let's eliminate the differences.

MARTIN DE PORRES

In Martin's time, the world in general debated the question of whether African slaves and those born of mixed racial parentage were even human. Additionally, the church debated whether such people possessed a redeemable soul. From his earliest days, Martin had settled this question for himself; he saw God as his heavenly father and devoted his life to love of this father and to service of all God's creatures. At the same time, Martin realized that others could not help seeing him as a "black mulatto dog," as he was often called. He gloried in this title since it affirmed his sense of sin and kinship with all God's creatures. Martin knew, as we in modern times sometimes fail to recognize, that we are all indeed sinners.

Another difference between the times is the austerity of life and the extremity of the penances practiced by Martin. Five hundred years ago, everyone's daily existence was physically far more difficult and demanding than life today. And penances such as the use of hair shirts and physical flagellation were common then for those working toward holiness. Martin's use of these practices was unusual only in the intensity of the love for Christ that motivated him.

In contrast, the similarities between Martin's day and our own are more pervasive than one would think. In the area around his birthplace in Lima, Peru, social injustice flourished. A system based on the prejudices of race and rank was rigorously imposed, pitting the rich against the poor and the oppressors against the weak. In 500 years, these conditions have not been overcome either in our own country or throughout the world. Undoubtedly, these conditions have led many people from oppressed backgrounds to flock to Martin, who has been named a patron of social justice. For this reason, each chapter ends with an invocation to Martin in English, Vietnamese, and Spanish. May Martin show us all the way to peace and justice in the midst of our increasing diversity.

CHAPTER ONE

BEGINNINGS

The Spirit of the Lord has been given to me
for he has anointed me…
to bring good news to the poor.

Isaiah 61:1

St. Martin de Porres, son of a Spanish nobleman and a freed African slave, was consumed by the love of God from an early age. He, in turn, poured out this love by serving all God's creatures, from mice to archbishops. Martin, named the *Apostle of Charity,* exemplifies what Christ intended when he called us to love others as he has loved us. To understand St. Martin de Porres and his extraordinary life, it is helpful to see him in the environment that was so important to his daily life.

Martin was born in December 1579, in Lima, Peru. His was a world that was as hostile to Christian virtue and values as is our present day world, so tortured with violence and injustices. His birth occurred just 34 years after the founding of the city by the conquistador, Francesco Pizarro. With the conquistadors came the sword, the crown of Spanish dominion, and the Catholic faith. And although baptism of the natives was the wish of the crown, the power of the sword, fired with a lust for the treasures of New Spain, dominated the conquerors of the land.

The Founding of Lima

Pizarro sailed into the port of Callao, five or six miles down the River Rimac from the site of a small native settlement. He had already established a capital in the Inca city of Jauja in the Andes Mountains, but since Jauja was inland, he wanted to establish a new capital with easy access to the Pacific Ocean. Near Callao was a city whose plaza Pizarro declared to be more spacious and splendid than any in Spain, and he promptly declared that city the new capital. Since he had arrived around the feast of Epiphany, celebrating the arrival of the kings at Bethlehem, he named the new capital the *City of Kings*. Had Pizarro been able to see just a few years into the future, he might have called it the *City of Saints* for so it was to become. During Martin's time, four other saints brought God's love to this city, filled with social injustice, avarice, and poverty. (See chapter eight.)

Later the City of Kings was renamed Lima, perhaps because of the lime trees that flourished there, perhaps because the natives said the name of the river Rimac with a soft "r" and the Spaniards pronounced the "r" as an "l" sound, making Rimac, Limac.

Furious battles with the Incas marked the rest of Pizarro's career until he was murdered in Lima in 1542.

At one point he held captive the Inca leader, demanding a ransom of a room filled with gold and another of silver for the Inca's release. In today's currency, this fortune alone would be worth more than $30 million. Over time, gold and silver jewelry and artworks taken from the Incas were melted down and sent to Spain as bars or ingots. The treasures of a nation were tossed into the furnace.

Lima, a Port City

The significance of Lima as a port city cannot be overlooked when trying to understand the environment in which Martin lived and labored his whole life. Spain sent two fleets a year to the New World. Necessities of flour, wine, and olive oil and luxuries of fine clothes and furniture were unloaded at Panama and transported across the isthmus by river and road. Then a Pacific fleet was loaded, and the goods were carried to Lima for use in the entire colony. For the return trip, the ships were loaded with the precious metals of silver, gold, and mercury and escorted by the Spanish navy to protect the cargo from pirates lurking along the coast. The heavy labor of loading and transporting goods across land was accomplished mostly by African and native slaves.

The People Of Lima

Both the battles for power and land, and the hunger for gold, silver, and mercury characterized the city into which Martin was born. Lima had a population of about 25,000, according to an incomplete census taken in 1613. As precious metals were melted, so the people of the city melted into many combinations of races, creating in the city distinct social classes. As Martin was growing up, the population consisted of four specific groups, although by the time of his birth about half of the population was mulatto, a mixture of races, or African.

First there were the Spanish, both officials and priests. Spaniards held most of the government offices, frequently purchased from the king of Spain, first Charles V and later Philip II. Because both kings were eager not only to colonize, but also to baptize Christians, many Spanish priests belonging to religious orders such as the Dominicans, Franciscans, Jesuits, and others soon flooded the city. (Dominicans, the Order Martin would join, were on the ships with Pizarro when he first landed.) Within 100 years, the population was estimated to be 10 percent clerics, that is, priests, friars, and lay brothers. Also at that time, one-third of the buildings in Lima belonged to the church. For the most part, Spaniards lived in ornate palaces, rode in fine carriages, and governed the city with political and religious laws.

Next in position were the Creoles, free Africans, and half-castes. Creoles were Spaniards who had been born in the New World. Spaniards had brought Africans to the New World as early as 1501. Some of them were now free as was Martin's mother, Ana Velazquez. Martin himself was a half-caste, and there were many varieties of these. Mulattos, like Martin, were a mixture of the white and African races. Mestizos were part Indian and part white. Chinos were part Indian and part African. From this mixed group came the skilled workers and the common labor force. These were the people who would build the churches and palaces of the city.

Added to this mix was the Spanish army (not counted in the census) that added approximately another 25,000 to the population. The army was dispatched from Lima to trouble spots up and down the Pacific coast of South America. The coastline of Peru itself is 1,400 miles long, and the new country was vast. These often ill-fed and underpaid troops were kept busy, ensuring that the native population labored for the conquerors and peacefully paid the heavy taxes levied by the crown and local officials.

Finally, there were African slaves and indigenous or native groups called Indians. Many of these natives had been frequently enslaved and exploited by the Incas, the dominant Indian group. Now they were treated no better by the Spaniards. Indians were often dragged from their homes, chained, and forced to work for a period of time in the mines. If they didn't perish when the mines collapsed, they often died of overwork, mistreatment, and Old World diseases such as small pox brought by the Spaniards. Still others died from the mercury and carbon dioxide poisons in the mines.

Ruling the City

The viceroy, appointed by the king, lived in Lima and ruled the new colony, which included all of South America except Portuguese Brazil. A series of viceroys built palaces, churches, and universities in the New World. The first university was San Marcos, founded by the Dominicans in 1513. The king of Spain sent laws to the viceroy governing taxation, products to be sent to Spain, and treatment of the natives, but these laws were frequently ignored.

Francesco de Toledo, the fifth viceroy, who ruled from 1569 to 1582, around the time of Martin's birth, tried to make many reforms in the government and in the treatment of the natives outside the city of Lima. But the viceroy who followed Toledo declared, "This land was founded upon greed and vested interest, and this is what they always worship." The actions of many lesser government officials led him to this sad declaration. Many of them had either purchased their positions or simply inherited them. By seeking their own welfare and ignoring attempts at more humanitarian treatment of the native Indians, these officials caused problems in the new colony. A native legend from this time says truly, "The world was turned upside down." In just a few years, Martin's life would provide a sharp contrast to this behavior and an example of how to turn the world right side up again.

Martin's Birth and Early Days

The few square miles of Lima, just south of the equator, are a kind of seaside desert at the foot of the Andes Mountains. Into this tempestuous, tormented city, Martin was born in 1579. His father, Juan de Porres, was a blue-eyed Spanish nobleman of the Order of

Alcantara, a religious and military order from Spain. In Panama, he met Martin's mother, Ana Velazquez, a talented and beautiful freed black. They traveled from Panama to Lima, whether together or separately is not known. Here Martin was born, followed two years later by his sister, Juana. Juan de Porres was working for the king, and laws forbade him from marrying an African. Many sources imply he was also unhappy that the children were dark like their mother instead of light complected as he was, although some sources suggest that Juana was lighter in color than Martin. Whether because of his dissatisfaction or because of an assignment from the king it is not known, but Juan soon left Lima. When Martin was baptized at Saint Sebastian Church in 1579, the baptismal record noted that his father was unknown.

Whatever money Juan left with Ana for herself and the care of the children was soon gone, and she was forced to find work. At an early age, Martin showed his intelligence and willingness to help, but his mother was frequently disappointed in how her young son ran his errands.

Sometimes his return home was delayed because he could seldom pass a church without stopping for a word with his heavenly father. He quickly learned that if he did not have an earthly father to protect him, he could rely on the love and mercy of his heavenly father. Since Lima had many churches, Martin often spent hours kneeling before the altar of one or another in silent prayer, forgetting his errands and worrying his mother who was waiting anxiously for his return.

At other times, when Ana gave him a few of her hard-earned coins to run to the market for bread, eggs, and fruit for their simple meals, Martin would set off with a basket on his arm to bring back food. Unfortunately, once he left their street (named *Espiritu Sant* or *Holy Spirit*), he often encountered someone poorer than his family. Even at this early age, his heart was moved by the needs of the poor, and he could not resist giving his mother's few coins to one of the beggars he met on his trip to the market. On his return, Martin would explain, "I met this poor Indian woman. She was blind and her husband and son have perished in the mines. She needed those few coins more than we do."

Martin knew that he, his sister, and his mother would have little or nothing to eat as a result of his charity. He knew his mother would be disappointed and justifiably angry. He also knew he would probably be punished. But still he could seldom resist the cry of the poor. Even his mother's tears and her punishments did not keep him from helping those he felt were in greater need. He accepted his punishment, and if he cried he did so because he had been disobedient and had displeased his mother. Already he was fulfilling his destiny to bring good news to the poor.

When Martin was eight and Juana just six, Juan de Porres returned to Lima. He was not in the city long before he learned of Martin's quick wit, goodness, and concern for the poor. Juan decided that his children should return with him to his government post in Guayaquil, in what is now Equador. Here Juan would acknowledge his children and provide them with an appropriate education.

MARTIN DE PORRES

Reflection

We live in a world that is larger and more complex than Martin's world. It is filled with people of different races and backgrounds that we must meet, work, and live with every day. Martin's love for the poor at this early age provides a model for us. Remembering that God's love for each single person is without end should lead us, as it did Martin, to look first to the needs of others and to serve others as well as we can.

Martin's early devotion to Our Lord in prayer through his frequent visits to churches was the inspiration for his love of others. If prayer is an important part of our life, we will remain close to Our Lord. We will remember always Our Lord's concern for the suffering and the poor, and this remembrance will guide us to works of love in his name.

St. Martin de Porres, pray for us.
Thánh Martin de Porres, caú cho chúng con.
San Martín de Porres, ruega por nosotros.

CHAPTER TWO

MARTIN'S EDUCATION AND EARLY LIFE

The child grew and became strong, filled with wisdom;
and the favor of God was upon him.

Luke 2:40

Leaving Ana behind, Juan de Porres, Martin, and Juana began their long journey to Guayaquil. The initial part of the trip, five or six miles to the harbor city of Callao, was an event in itself. The children and their father rode in a grand carriage as befitted a government official. At the harbor, they saw fine sailing vessels being loaded with gold and silver for their return to Spain. And here young Martin, perhaps for the first time, saw the African and Indian slaves laboring with bent backs to get the precious cargo on the ship. Finally, the three boarded their own ship that would take them many miles up the coast to what is now Ecuador.

A Tutor Is Hired

Once they arrived in Guayaquil, Martin's father hired a tutor to provide a suitable education for the children. Although little is known of that education, at this early age their daily instructions were probably limited to reading, writing, and doing sums. No doubt their reading included scripture. As the children were tutored, their natural intelligence was given a chance to shine.

Life for them in Guayaquil was very different from life in Lima. For example, they were dressed as befitted the wards of an important government official, and they ate like royalty. Also, Juan de Porres spent time with them himself. He was now willing to call the two children his own, as is evident from the fact that he introduced himself as their father to his uncle, Diego de Miranda. But living in luxury was not something that Martin enjoyed. Fortunately for him, this phase of his education ended after a few years when Juan was transferred to a government post in Panama. Juana went to live with her great uncle, de Miranda, and Martin returned to a new life in Lima.

A New Direction Is Chosen

Before they parted, one of the things Martin and his father discussed was Martin's future. At that time, young men who were not of the privileged upper class continued their education by serving as an apprentice or helper to a skilled craftsman or professional. Many choices were open to Martin because of his father's influence.

"Martin," his father undoubtedly said, "when you return to Lima, you must learn a trade so that you will not be dependent on your mother. Would you like to learn to be a carpenter? You are clever with your hands, and people always need the services of a carpenter."

Martin shook his head.

"The Spanish have brought many horses to Lima. Would you like to become a blacksmith and learn to shoe horses?"

"I love animals, Father, but I would like to be of more service to Our Lord," Martin replied.

"Perhaps you would like to work with stone and help build the new churches and palaces that will be needed as the city grows," his father suggested. "Our Lord is pleased with beautiful churches built to honor him."

"That would be a great privilege, Father, but I have already thought about what I would like to do. I would like to learn to be a barber."

A barber at that time did much more than cut hair. He was the doctor of those days, the one to whom people came for healing in sickness, for setting of broken bones, and for being operated on, simple and rudimentary as surgery then was. Martin saw in this profession an opportunity to fulfill his desire to be of service to others.

So when Martin, now about 12, returned to Lima, he was apprenticed to Dr. Marcelo de Rivero, a barber surgeon who would teach him the skills of cutting hair and beards and, more importantly, all the skills necessary for caring for the sick. After spending a few days with his mother, Martin moved to a boarding house that would be closer to de Rivero and also closer to the Church of San Lázaro.

New Routines

Martin's days were soon spent in a happy routine. Rising before daybreak to attend Mass and often serving the priest as an acolyte prepared his heart for the coming day. Then he would walk to de Rivero's shop and begin his duties. He quickly learned to cut hair properly and in due time began to assist de Rivero as he tended to the sick. Because of his intelligence and diligence, Martin soon learned to make medicines from natural herbs and administer to the sick as well as the good doctor, who found in Martin an exceptional student.

Martin accepted no wages for his services except for what was needed for his room and board. If a few extra coins came into his hands, they were soon given to lighten the load for one of the poor. Fortunately, his mother did not need his help since she was comfortably taken care of from the time Juan de Porres had finally acknowledged his family.

Nights of Prayer

After a long day of learning potions, herbs, and bandages to relieve the distress and pain of patients, Martin would return to the home of his landlady, Ventura de

Luna. He took his supper with Ventura although even at this early age he ate little more than bread and a piece of fruit. Ventura soon became very fond of Martin, depending on him for small tasks around the house that she could not do herself. One day she asked him, "Will you plant a lemon tree in the side yard for me?"

Martin planted the tree, and it grew and flourished, bearing fruit year-round for several hundred years. After his death, visitors would stop by to view "Martin's Tree." This was the first of many that Martin later planted around the countryside. Maybe he was hearing Christ's cry on the cross, "I thirst." These trees provided lemons, oranges, and other fruit to ease the thirst and hunger of weary travelers and the poor.

Because of his friendly relationship with Ventura, Martin felt free to ask her for her discarded candle stubs for light in the evening. He asked to take the stubs to his room. Since he often repeated this request, and because Ventura saw a light shining in Martin's room, she became curious. What was he doing with a light so late at night? When she peeked through the keyhole, she saw Martin in prayer before his crucifix, his arms stretched out like Christ's and his face covered with tears. Martin was fervent in prayer for long hours, only to rise early the next morning to assist at Mass and begin anew a long day learning his trade.

The sight of the young boy in prayer was so inspiring that Ventura could not keep her secret to herself and shared it with her neighbors. Sometimes she even invited close friends to observe Martin as well. Those in the neighborhood were soon convinced of Martin's holiness. This early devotion to Our Lord and his

Blessed Mother brought Martin many graces, not the least of which was the peaceful serenity with which he approached those who needed his help.

Martin Proves His Skill

Dr. de Rivero was pleased with Martin's progress in the healing arts and realized that he could leave the infirmary in the boy's care, especially when his duties called him elsewhere. One day while Martin was working alone, a woman frantically rushed into the office calling for Dr. de Rivero.

"He is not here," Martin said, "but surely I can help."

The woman was terribly upset. She had rushed ahead of those who were carrying an Indian who had been wounded in a street fight. Realizing Martin's youth, she exclaimed, "How can you help? You're just a boy."

When the others arrived carrying their wounded friend, Martin set to work. Quickly he mixed a special remedy to cleanse the wound. He stopped the flow of blood and wrapped the wound carefully in a clean bandage. When he had finished, he offered the poor Indian a drink of wine to comfort him. Although the woman and the other Indians had at first been reluctant to accept the services of the young mulatto, they were all soon singing his praises, especially when their friend was able to return quickly to work. Word of his ability soon spread as the Indians told their friends that Martin was as good as the doctor in healing. Soon others came to the infirmary requesting that Martin,

with his unfailing smile and gentle manner, be the one to minister to them.

The days and months flowed into years and Martin was soon 15. Although he loved his work, he wanted to dedicate his life to God. He had long admired the Dominicans in their flowing white habits and thought that, if he could only serve these holy men, he would be truly happy. After many discussions with the Dominican priest to whom he confided his wishes, Martin determined to present himself as a servant to the priests and brothers.

When Juan de Porres heard of his son's intention, he demanded that Martin be received in the order at least as a lay brother. Juan's position and importance might have achieved this, but Martin wished only to serve as the lowest of the low, attached to the Order as a servant or a *donado*. As a servant, he would have a place to sleep in the monastery, would eat with the priests and brothers, and would wear the white habit of the Dominicans and a black cape. But he would not wear the full habit, nor would he take the vows common to religious. Martin, of course, had his own promise to keep and was overjoyed to be drawing closer to his beloved Lord.

Reflection

Martin's dedication to his task of learning to care for the sick and injured continued his development. This education was important and would serve him well in the monastery. Trying to learn new skills and to do a job well are tasks we are given each day. Being faithful in prayer, as Martin was, will give us the strength and courage we need to accomplish whatever God calls us to do.

St. Martin de Porres, pray for us.
Thánh Martin de Porres, caú cho chúng con.
San Martín de Porres, ruega por nosotros.

CHAPTER THREE

GROWING IN VIRTUE

And over all these put on love, that is, the bond of perfection.
Colossians 3:14

Martin's visits to neighborhood churches as a young boy and his long nights of prayer as a teenager began his spiritual life. His devotion to Mary and to his crucified Savior became the source of his humility and the fountain from which overflowed his charity. This charity would come to embrace all God's creatures. Martin could not view the consequences of sin, the sufferings of Christ, without holding himself responsible. If Christ could humble himself to death on the cross for love, shouldn't Martin, a mere creature of God, also strive to humble himself? If Christ could humble himself to wash the feet of the apostles for love, shouldn't Martin humble himself to serve the Dominican priests and brothers in whatever way he could? Martin's answer was "Yes!"

Once accepted as a lowly servant in the *convento* or monastery by the prior provincial, Juan de Lorenzana, Martin enthusiastically embraced his life with the Dominicans. He attended daily Mass, often serving at Mass. He studied the Rule of St. Augustine, the Rule that provided directions for the brothers and priests to govern their lives in ways that would help them draw closer to God. The Rule and the Constitutions of the Order prescribed places and times for silence, places and times for prayer. They described the wool habit that Martin would cherish, and above all they advised obedience to one's superiors. Since Martin accepted all members of the Order as his superiors, he found many ways to practice love and humility. Although being just a servant, not bound to observe the Rule, Martin found it a joy to do so.

Early Duties

At first, Martin's duties were to sweep the corridors, cloisters, and cells clean of the dust and debris that blew in from the streets. Pictures today often depict Martin with his broom in his hands. Cleaning toilets in the days before indoor plumbing was no pleasant task, but one he fulfilled with the cheerful smile he brought to all his work. He knew that in performing these tasks to the best of his ability, he was pleasing Our Lord. If others criticized his work, Martin was quick to accept the rebuke and acknowledge his fault. For example, if someone called him a black dog or a mulatto unfit to sweep their sacred halls, Martin thanked him. He told the one who corrected him, "You have only spoken the truth. Please forgive this miserable sinner."

From our perspective some 400 years later, one might wonder about the harsh words often directed at Martin from the priests, brothers, and students in the monastery. First, it must be remembered that most of these men were Spanish. At home in Spain, as in all of Europe, the king and high-church leaders were still struggling with whether blacks such as Martin were human or even possessed a soul. Further, even good people sometimes have difficulty when faced with someone of Martin's holiness, patience, and good will. As for Martin, his willingness to accept humiliation should not be judged by our standards as masochism or abject servility. Rather, he had a heightened sense of both the sacredness of the religious life and his own sinfulness as a human being, something modern Christians have lost over the centuries.

Martin's humility and devotion to Our Lord is exemplified by an incident that occurred some years later. Martin had been invited to the home of the visiting archbishop of Mexico, Don Feliciano de Vega, who was ill and asked Martin to stay and take care of him. During this time, one of the brothers found Martin back in the monastery doing his usual morning task of cleaning the toilets.

"Why are you doing this filthy and thankless task when you could be in the palace of the archbishop?" the brother asked.

Echoing the words of the psalmist, Martin answered, "I would rather spend a few hours here in the house of my Lord than spend days in a palace."

The Community Barber

Because he had learned to be a skillful barber, his superior soon assigned him to cut the hair of the approximately 300 priests and brothers who lived in the monastery. Often he no sooner finished the job of cutting everyone's hair when it was time to begin again. The task was not only time consuming and thankless, but often a source of conflict. The Rule described the haircut to be short in the back and on the sides. Not all of the Dominicans were satisfied with the prescribed cut and wished their hair cut according to their individual preferences.

One day Brother Santiago arrived for his haircut shortly before the time for evening prayers. As he placed himself in the chair, he began to read a book he had brought along.

"Please hurry, Martin; I do not wish to be late for prayers," he said.

Martin began the task carefully, following the letter of the Rule for haircuts. He finished just in time for evening prayer. Brother Santiago, who was a little vain, looked at his hair and raged, "You know I like my hair long in the back and on the sides. You stupid dog, why did you cut the back and the sides so short? Don't you know anything about how to cut hair?"

Martin answered quietly, "I am sorry I have offended you, but I cut your hair as the Rule prescribed." With soft answers and a smile, he continually accepted rebukes for his work as a barber until at last all, including Brother Santiago, accepted the haircut prescribed by the Rule and administered by Martin.

MARTIN DE PORRES

Martin's Love of His Dominican Habit

Martin loved his Dominican habit, described in the Rule as to be made of white serge, rough wool. Of the habits available in the monastery, he always chose the most worn and tattered. When someone was ready to discard his habit because it was patched beyond repair, Martin accepted it readily. As the least important person in the community, he felt the patched and threadbare garment was most suitable for him. His sister, Juana, wanted to provide him with a second habit. He refused. "I can wash this one and put it on again. I have no need for a second habit."

At one point, for some reason, wool to make new habits was difficult to find. Apparently no one had yet perfected the making of wool from the llamas that were plentiful in Peru, so habits began to be made of a much softer linen cloth. Martin was concerned. His devotion to the Rule sent him from the monastery to beg for money and to visit all the tradesmen in Lima. His efforts were rewarded with enough wool serge to clothe all in the community with the required white serge habits.

Not wanting to offend the others, Martin managed to quietly replace the linen garments when they came to the laundry. As a linen habit was laundered, he replaced it with the prescribed woolen habit.

Martin freely chose to spend his life serving the Dominicans. His love for the Order was never more evident than on the day he heard that the prior was taking treasured pictures from the church to sell because money was in short supply for food and other necessities for the community.

As the priest trudged along the streets to the marketplace, Martin caught up with him. "Please, Father, do not sell these beautiful pictures of the saints. If the *convento* requires money, sell me as a slave. I am strong and willing and should bring a good price."

The good priest was astounded at the offer. What humility and dedication to the Order the young man showed!

"Martin, we will never be so poor that we would sell you," he answered. "Your shining, joyful face brings us the richest of blessings. That is a treasure that money can't buy."

Prayer and Penance

After this, Martin returned to the monastery with renewed zeal for prayer. As he grew in holiness, he added austere penances daily. His nightly vigils before the cross continued, and to this he added beating himself with a whip, sometimes to the point of blood. He bound his body with a tight chain that cut into his flesh. If the beatings, the chain, and the hair shirt he wore under his habit seem extreme penances today, it is important to remember that these practices were common in the sixteenth century. In addition, Martin continued the habit of his youth of eating little and never meat. The final three days of Holy Week he fasted completely. His love of God and his sense of his own sinfulness fired him with the desire to do ever more prayer and reparation for his sins and the sins of others.

Beginning to Work in the Infirmary

At one time, a terrible epidemic swept through the city of Lima. Many in the city became ill, and more than 60 of the residents of the monastery were also afflicted. Knowing that Martin had special talents in healing the sick, the prior added to his duties the care of the sick in the infirmary. Martin was tireless in attending to them. Whenever patients needed a drink of water or their head or hands cooled with a towel, Martin was there. He seemed to be in all places at once, day and night, and always at the bedside of anyone who wanted him. The sick can be difficult and demanding. Martin, however, found his duties especially fulfilling. He treated each person in the infirmary as if the patient were his Lord, remembering Jesus' words, "I was sick and you visited me."

Charity More Important than Obedience

Although humility and obedience were important virtues in Martin's life, charity was always more important, from the times as a child when he had given his mother's few coins to the poor. Martin often rescued the sick and the dying he met on his journeys outside the *convento* and brought them to his simple cell to treat them until they were well enough to leave. Several in the monastery had complained about this practice, and Martin was called to see his superior.

"Martin, you must stop bringing sick vagrants to your cell. You may be bringing dirt and diseases into the monastery."

"Yes, Father," Martin agreed, "I will stop bringing the sick to my cell." A few days later as Martin was on an errand outside the monastery, he came upon a poor Indian who had been wounded in a fight. If Martin left the man at the side of the road, he would surely die. Perhaps thinking of the story of the Good Samaritan, Martin knew he could not leave the man there. He helped him to his feet and supported him as he walked him to his cell in the monastery. Martin washed his wound, applied some herbs, and bandaged the wound.

Someone who knew of the superior's warning to stop bringing the sick and wounded into the monastery witnessed Martin assisting the man to his cell and immediately reported Martin's disobedience. Martin was called to explain.

"I forbid you to bring any more of these vagrants into the monastery, Martin. Now you must accept a penance for your disobedience."

"I accept the penance, Reverend Father. I am sorry that I have failed in obedience." Martin humbly bowed his head and continued, "I weighed obedience against charity and decided charity was more important."

Making Final Profession

When Martin had arrived at the monastery, he had intended to remain always as a simple servant, a *donado*, a gift to the Order. And although his father, Juan de Porres, had wanted Martin accepted as a brother, Martin had refused this. It was just as well that he accepted and rejoiced in his position as a donado. The Order would have been reluctant to issue that kind of welcome because of the ongoing debate about Africans' humanity and soul, as well as the specific matter of Martin's illegitimacy. These were both strong reasons at that time for refusing to admit him to full acceptance in the Order. In spite of this, because of Martin's humility, obedience, and devotion to prayer, his superiors were eager to have him more closely united with the Order.

After nine years, when Martin was 24 years old, his superiors felt that his example of holiness and devotion to the Rule were reasons for insisting that he make perpetual vows, so that he would remain always with the Order. It has long been assumed that Martin was a member of the Order as a lay brother. However, new research suggests this may not have been the case, and that he was a *hermano donado,* one permanently tied to the Order as a "kind" of brother (*hermano* is translated here to mean *blood brother*). This confusion led to the assumption that Martin was professed as a lay brother.

Whatever his exact status, Martin's profession was recorded in the priory's books of professions on June 2, 1603. It is clear that he pledged to spend the rest of his life serving his Lord with the Dominicans. It was a day of great joy both for Martin and the community, which was to be glorified by his presence.

Reflection

Martin's ready obedience, his spirit of prayer and penance, his acceptance of humiliating duties and embarrassing taunts are an example for all of us. At some time, we have all endured harsh words and unkind actions. Martin's example should help us to accept injustice with dignity. We can love and pray for those who humiliate us. Even the lesson that sometimes obedience must yield to the greater call of charity can be a guide for our actions.

St. Martin de Porres, pray for us.
Thánh Martin de Porres, caú cho chúng con.
San Martín de Porres, ruega por nosotros.

CHAPTER FOUR

MARTIN SERVES HIS COMMUNITY

The fruit of love is service, which is compassion in action.
Mother Teresa

After Martin made his profession to remain perpetually a Dominican *donado,* one might expect that his life changed greatly, but it didn't. He went about his daily duties with the same smile and gracious manner as before, but the love that filled his heart inspired him to even greater acts of service. The Dominican ideal is devotion to truth. Martin announced the truth daily by proclaiming with his every action the truth of God's love for all.

Daily Duties

Each morning Martin climbed the tower of the church to ring the bell to announce the prayer to Our Lady, the Angelus. This did not happen only in the monastery.

MARTIN DE PORRES

Bells all over Lima rang out to call people to begin their day with a prayer to Mary, Jesus' mother. Before Martin left his cell to ring the bell, he would lift his mind and heart to God. The crucifix in his cell, along with a picture of Mary and one of St. Dominic, helped him focus his mind and body on serving his Lord to his best ability.

Next, Martin served at a Mass either in the Church of the Holy Rosary or at one of the side chapels. Serving a priest at Mass had been a special joy for Martin since his boyhood. Because people in those times did not receive holy communion at every Mass they attended, he especially relished those days on which he could receive Our Lord in the Holy Eucharist.

Martin could normally receive communion on Sundays and special feast days. After Mass on those special occasions, he disappeared to spend a few hours in prayerful thanksgiving. Everyone in the community knew it was a hopeless task to try to find Martin until his thanksgiving was completed. They would look in his cell and in hidden corners of the monastery, but he could not be found. There was, however, one sure way to find him if he was truly needed. If his superior called for Martin, he would immediately appear in response to the call of obedience.

Martin's days were spent much as they had always been—sweeping or cleaning. Perhaps he would be in the garden, tending the vegetables and special herbs he used in the infirmary or gathering flowers for the church's altar. Much of his time was spent in the infirmary caring for the sick. But no matter where he was or what duties he was fulfilling, Martin remained in the presence of his beloved God and performed his work for love of his brothers.

One of his special duties required him to be responsible for the materials used in the infirmary. Sheets, blankets, and mattresses were in short supply and each was always accounted for. Even worn sheets were not discarded but were torn up for bandages. One day an outsider who had come to Martin for treatment was left alone for a few minutes. Seeing a basket of sheets nearby, he decided to help himself and stuffed a sheet into his baggy trousers.

When Martin returned, he judged the man well enough to leave. As the man turned to go, Martin spoke gently to him. "You have taken a sheet that is much needed for our sick." His face aflame with shame, the man returned the sheet, wondering as he did so how Martin had known of his theft.

On another occasion, a cot was stolen from the infirmary. Martin knew exactly who had taken it and where he could find it, and he went immediately to recover it. His vigilance in taking care of the goods belonging to the infirmary was not particularly remarkable since that was his duty. What was remarkable was Martin's knowledge of things that were being stolen and his ability to restore the items without wasting time or words or causing offense to others.

He could turn a critical judgment to a lesson in charity. Once as he was talking of spiritual matters to an elderly priest, their attention was diverted when a young religious passed them. The young priest was wearing a pair of shiny, fashionable shoes. The older priest was upset.

"Did you see those shoes?" he asked. "Such expensive shoes are not appropriate for a Dominican."

Martin understood the older priest's dismay but was able to see the shoes in a different light. "Yes, those shoes are not what you or I would wear. But God may use those shoes to draw a sinner to confession. A sinner might be turned away by our somewhat tattered appearance, but he would know that a priest wearing those shoes would understand his failings." And Martin smiled.

At the proceedings for his beatification some 20 years after his death, many of those who had known Martin testified to his beautiful smile. No matter what task he was performing, Martin's face was always wreathed in a special smile, one that affirmed the presence in his soul of special grace. Holiness radiates, and Martin's smile radiated and spread warmth and comfort to those around him. When he was suffering, either from physical pain or from pain inflicted by others, his smile was even more luminous.

Caring for the Sick

Many stories were told of Martin's care and cures when tending the sick in the infirmary. For example, one of the priests was unable to use his arms or legs. To be completely paralyzed is a terrible affliction, but it also meant that he could no longer perform his duties as a priest. This must have been devastating to him, as his mind was still clear. To add to his pain, he was unable to speak and explain his needs to those who were caring for him.

Observing the priest's pain and frustration, Martin asked others to pray that God would restore at least the priest's ability to speak and to use his hands to feed himself. Martin also prayed. Although the priest was still paralyzed, he was overcome with joy to find he was able to talk and use his hands again. Martin, of course, attributed the cure to the prayer of others, not his own.

Sometimes his advice to the sick was only common sense. One brother who was having difficulty sleeping implored Martin to stay with him until he could sleep. Martin said, "If you will only place your bed between the door and the window, you will be able to fall asleep." Certainly this advice was common sense for sleeping on a hot subtropical night before air-conditioning existed.

At other times, Martin's advice to the sick was a little out of the ordinary. Brother Andreas had been suffering with a fever and congestion in his lungs. When he asked Martin for help, he received strange advice. "Wait until evening and then take a bath in the pool just outside the cloister."

Although he was tempted to ignore the advice, Brother Andreas felt so ill he decided he was ready to try anything. Late in the evening he dove into the water, which was shockingly cold. He stayed in the pool so long that he was almost unable to move. Fortunately, someone came along and pulled him out, dried him off, and sent him to bed. Curing a fever and bad lungs with a plunge in cold water is not what most doctors would recommend, but the next day, Brother

Andreas was well. His fever was gone and he was able to breathe easily.

Brother Christobel was suffering after he had had a tooth pulled by someone other than Martin. A dry socket, which can form after a tooth has been extracted, can be extremely painful. Martin visited the young man and tapped his cheek lightly. Then he stuffed a piece of bread in the cavity. The pain was immediately relieved. However, during the night the ferocious pain returned.

Brother Christobel sat on his bed weeping and wishing that Martin could return to help him. But it was late at night and no one was about. Suddenly, when he was almost despairing, Martin appeared, tapped his cheek gently again, and comforted him saying, "This pain will not last forever. Let me look again." Then he removed the stitches and the pain disappeared. Brother Christobel knew he had been healed by the touch of Martin's hand, but Martin insisted it was the simple removal of the stitches.

One of Martin's most serious cases was that of Father Pedro whose leg had become infected and turned gangrenous. The leg would soon have to be amputated. Martin visited Father Pedro the afternoon before the surgery. He removed the bandages and bathed the leg carefully. Next he prepared a small salad from vegetables he had just picked from the garden. The priest was grateful for the attention in spite of the pain his swollen leg was giving him, and he ate the salad with gratitude.

The next morning when Martin visited him, Father Pedro was walking joyfully around his bed. When he saw Martin, he exclaimed, "You have cured me. My leg is healed!"

Martin never admitted that his attentions had ever effected a cure. He had prayed for Father Pedro, changed his bandages, and prepared him a salad, but made no claim for anything else. Smiling with his own joy at the cure, Martin said, "If you are now well, it is only because God has more work for you."

But despite Martin's many healings and despite his now being perpetually gifted to the Order, the harsh treatment he had suffered in the past did not cease altogether. While he was attending a very sick religious, Martin had to move the man and in so doing caused him pain. The priest cried out, "What are you doing, you stupid black dog! You should not be allowed near anyone who is ill."

Martin, upset at having caused pain, immediately knelt beside the bed to beg forgiveness. "I am sorry I hurt you. You are right to criticize me. I am not worthy to even kiss your hands, which hold the body of Christ each morning."

Extraordinary Gifts

God graced Martin with special gifts to help him in caring for all the sick, both in the infirmary and throughout the monastery. Martin knew who would benefit most from his care. He knew who would appreciate a piece of fruit from the garden and who needed his pillow fluffed and a sprig of the medicinal herb rosemary placed by his head. Once a sick friar asked for an orange, and Martin soon returned with one. The next day the friar was well enough to realize that oranges were not in season. He had to ponder where Martin had found the fruit.

Frequently, even in the middle of the night, Martin would appear beside the bed of one who was sick, as he had to Brother Christobel. He could also somehow pass through locked doors to provide comfort. He would bathe a fevered brow, change sheets, and do whatever was needed to make the long night in a sick bed more bearable.

Inevitably, however, some of his patients would be called home to heaven. Martin seemed to know who was in danger of dying and who was not. One day when making his rounds, he quickly summoned a priest to bring the Last Sacrament for Brother Lorenzo. Although elderly and with many weaknesses, Brother Lorenzo was still up and about, attempting to do his duties, and no one expected him to die. But die he did, soon after the Sacrament had been administered.

On the other hand, Brother Fernando was thought by all to be dying. He had received the Last Sacrament and the community, according to Dominican custom, had assembled at his door to sing the *Salve Regina,* a hymn to Mary. Martin assured the others that Brother Fernando would not die, and he did not. In a few days, he was well enough to return to his tasks.

The story of Brother Tomas' death is an unusual one. Brother Fernando was with him when he died, but Martin was elsewhere. Martin was then summoned to prepare Brother Tomas for burial while the other Dominicans remained in the hallway praying.

Martin questioned Brother Fernando, "Are you sure he has died?"

"Of course, I'm sure, but I will check his pulse one more time."

Martin knelt and began to pray before the small crucifix in the cell. Soon he rose to his feet and left the cell to announce to the waiting Dominicans, "Brother Tomas has not died. He is sitting up and asking for something to eat. In a few days he should be much better." And he was.

Reflection

It would seem that Martin's days were filled with wonderful cures and extraordinary events such as having special knowledge, walking through locked doors, and having an insight into the future. It must be remembered, however, that Martin spent 45 years with the Dominicans, and much of that time must have been filled with ordinary and humdrum activities such as we experience each day.

We may not have the great faith of Martin that permitted him to "move mountains" as our Lord promised, but we can accomplish our daily duties with love and dedication. Striving to remain always in the presence of God is a good beginning. Facing both the good and the bad of each day with a ready smile, as Martin did, is a goal we all can reach.

MARTIN DE PORRES

St. Martin de Porres, pray for us.
Thánh Martin de Porres, cáu cho chúng con.
San Martín de Porres, ruega por nosotros.

CHAPTER FIVE

A SPECIAL FRIEND TO NOVICES

*Therefore, brothers, stand firm
and hold fast to the traditions that you were taught.*
2 Thessalonians 2:15

Martin had a special relationship with the novices of the Order, young men who were learning about the rules and traditions of the Dominicans. Some of them would become priests and others would become brothers, but none of them had yet made a profession of vows. They were in some ways like the tender plants that Martin cared for in the garden, delicate and precious but needing training and direction to eventually produce fruit. Martin delighted in their company and helped them in many ways.

His Encouragement to Study

Martin assisted the novices in their studies in a variety of ways. Although he could not preach from the pulpit,

he could preach by his example. Also, as a servant of all, he took on the duty of seeing that student novices had the time needed for study. He did everything he could to free them from the concerns of daily living. He saw that their laundry was done and that their supplies—pen, ink, paper, and even books—were ready for them.

Long hours of study can be difficult, especially for the young. If one or another of the novices was not devoting himself enough, Martin was there to offer encouragement and to prod the slacker to more diligence. He explained that the glory of the Order depended on the novice's attention and devotion to the work of study.

On one occasion, Martin met two students who were discussing a weighty question about the perfection of essence (the intrinsic nature) and existence (the state of being) in God. They turned to Martin to ask his opinion. Martin replied, "Does not St. Thomas say that existence is more perfect than essence, but that in God essence and existence are one?" St. Thomas Aquinas was a great Dominican and a doctor of the church. He wrote the *Summa Theologica,* an explanation of Catholic philosophy and theology that is dozens of volumes in length.

The novices were astounded. That a humble servant could quote St. Thomas was nothing short of amazing. When they checked with their professor, he assured them, "Not only is Brother Martin correct, his knowledge is the 'science of saints.'" The professor realized that Martin must have possessed special knowledge and wisdom granted by God to the saintly, because it is unlikely that Martin had studied or even read the *Summa.*

At another time when the students were heatedly arguing another theological point, Martin asked them the reason for their loud and boisterous discussion. Again, he gave them a specific reference to the *Summa Theologica*. "If you will consult St. Thomas," he said, "you will find the answer to your argument." And then he gave them directions to the pertinent passage. But as the novices discovered, Martin's knowledge was not limited to just religious and theological matters, nor to the whereabouts of infirmary supplies.

Correcting with Kindness

After studying, several students had gone to Martin's cell in search of him, as he'd promised them a special treat after they completed their studies. Not finding Martin, they helped themselves to some fruit he kept for them in a drawer. One of the novices reached further into the drawer and discovered a coin Martin had intended for the poor. Glancing about to be sure no one observed him, he placed the coin in his shoe. When Martin returned, he was happy to see they had enjoyed the fruit. After a short talk about spiritual matters, the novices began to leave.

As they reached the door, Martin said, "One of you has taken something that does not belong to you."

The students looked at one another with dismay. Who would take something from Martin who was always so generous to them? And what would Martin have of any value anyway? Each protested in all innocence that he had taken nothing. Finally, Martin was forced to face the culprit and say, "The coin you have hidden in your shoe is intended for the poor. Please return it."

The student, blushing with shame, removed the coin and returned it. Martin, with his characteristic gentleness, said no more. But the novices left in wonder at his knowledge of the hidden coin.

It is often the way of the young to tease their peers for their weaknesses. Novices were no different. Poor Brother Cypriano was a favorite target of their teasing. Nephew of the archbishop, he was both short and fat. In addition, he was not a good student although he tried hard to learn. Fearing that the youth was being taunted to the point of giving up his vocation, Martin spoke to the other novices.

"Stop teasing Brother Cypriano. He is loved by God as you all are. Soon he will astonish you by his appearance and learning. He is destined to hold a high place in the Order and in the church."

Soon after this gentle correction, Brother Cypriano became quite ill. Martin was by his side and attended him carefully. After he recovered, Brother Cypriano was found to have grown twelve inches and was no longer overweight. He also improved remarkably in his studies. He was ordained a priest and later in life would become a bishop. He never forgot Martin's loving protection and help. The mulatto became for him, as for many of the novices, a model of the holiness he hoped to attain.

Good Times with the Novices

The master of novices, Father Andreas de Lison, recognized early not only Martin's holiness but also his good influence on the novices and was always delighted when he could allow the students a short time away from their studies in Martin's care. One of their special delights was to go with Martin to Limatambo, a country retreat where the Dominicans of Lima went to rest and relax away from the noise and confusion of the city.

In the fresh air and sunshine the novices played games, enjoyed a picnic lunch, and talked to Martin about spiritual matters. Martin, like his patron St. Dominic, constantly spoke either of God or to God so the conversation was always uplifting. Once, the relaxation was so enjoyable that everyone lost track of time, including Martin. As dusk began to fall, they realized that they could not travel the several miles to Lima before the city gates were locked. Further, the Rule prescribed that novices must be inside the *convento* before nightfall.

Somehow Martin managed to get everyone back within the city and then the monastery walls before nightfall. How they covered so many miles, the novices never knew, but they were grateful once again for the wonderful powers of their holy friend, Brother Martin.

Helping Novices with Temptations

Despite such pleasant breaks, the life of novices was difficult, and many of them suffered temptations regarding their vocations. Several stories illustrate Martin's care and concern for these youths. One evening Father Andreas came to find Martin.

"Two of the novices appear to have left the monastery without permission," he said. "I fear they are leaving for good. Can you help?"

Stopping only to pray for guidance and to ask the prior's permission to leave the monastery since it was already night, Martin set out to find the two fugitives. Somehow he knew they had headed for a nearby barn where they could spend the night. When he found them there, he spoke to them gently about the scripture story of the father's love for his prodigal son. Then Martin encouraged them to return to the monastery to take up again the cross of their daily duties. The novices were so moved by his words that they wondered how they could ever have abandoned their vocation.

By this time it was late at night and the doors to the *convento* were locked. Martin and the two prodigals entered through the locked doors and were soon safe in their cells. The next morning Martin reported their return to the master of novices. No one else would ever know of their ill-considered flight. They spent the rest of their lives as good and holy religious in the Order.

Brother Francisco, a Spanish youth of the nobility, was a more difficult case. Because of his vanity, he had often harassed Martin about the kind of haircut he wanted. But as always, Martin showed great love to those who called him names and insulted him. He frequently sent the young Francisco fresh fruit, not to appease him, but rather to express gratitude that the youth recognized Martin as the unworthy sinner he felt himself to be.

Sometime later, Brother Francisco was thinking of leaving the Order to accept an important position in

Lima as secretary of the treasury. Only Martin was aware of his temptation. He appeared beside the young man while he was on his way with others to dinner. In strong words, Martin told Francisco that he knew his thoughts of abandoning his vocation. Further, Martin warned him, "Believe me, what you were unwilling to do out of love of God, you will do out of fear of him."

As Francisco sat down to eat, he was overcome with a high fever and shivers. He asked permission to leave and go to bed. As he lay sick and shaking with fever, he thought about what Martin had said to him and gave up his plans to leave the monastery.

Just a month later, he began to think again of the wealth and privileges that would be his if he left the Order. Again he was stricken with a high fever. Once more he recovered, and once more he made plans to leave. Again the fever returned. This time it was so severe that he was at the point of death. The doctors despaired of saving him. There was nothing they could do. Francisco was given the Last Sacraments, then the door to his room was locked for the night. This was done on medical advice because the doctors feared someone would give him water, which would only make his condition worse.

Martin, for whom locked doors were no obstacle, appeared at his side. He freshened Francisco's bed, lightly sponged his body, changed his fever-soaked garments, and left a sprig of rosemary with him. Before he left, Francisco asked fearfully, "Will I die?"

Martin returned the question with a question, "Do you want to die?"

"No," was the response.

"Then you will not," was Martin's firm answer.

The next day all signs of Francisco's illness had disappeared. In a few days, when he was completely recovered, the doctors declared it a miracle. The real miracle was that Francisco was finally able to recognize that God was determined to save his vocation with the Dominicans, and that Martin had been right with his early warning.

Martin's Own Temptations

Besides helping the novices, Martin had to deal with his own temptations. But when one is so saintly, temptations are often of a more intense nature. Martin's vocation was never a cause for his concern, but he suffered battles with the devil himself. One night he was physically thrown around his cell and hurled against the wall by an unseen force. The noise of the brutal attack was such that others hastened to see what the trouble was. Martin was overheard to say, "What have you come here for? This is not your cell. Get out."

Then a fire broke out in his room. An officer of the guard rushed in to help put out the fire. Martin survived, and in the morning there were no signs of the struggle. He cautioned those who had witnessed the fight not to speak of it.

Another time Martin was climbing a back ladder to the infirmary. This back passageway was usually closed because it was unsafe, but he was in a hurry to attend to one of the sick. He was carrying clean sheets and a candle to light his way. Suddenly, he found himself face to face with the devil. Again, Martin asked with anger, "What are you doing here? Leave."

To hasten the devil's departure, Martin removed his belt and struck the devil with it. Then taking his candle, he burned two crosses in the wall. The next day, he saw to it that a 5-foot wooden cross was placed over those he had made. From then on the passage was safe, and others no longer feared to use it.

Reflection

We cannot find our way through locked doors, know the inmost thoughts of others, or cure the sick as Martin did so often. What we can do, however, is remain close to Our Father in thought, prayer, and conversation and try as much as possible to be a good example to others.

St. Martin de Porres, pray for us.
Thánh Martin de Porres, caú cho chúng con.
San Martín de Porres, ruega por nosotros.

CHAPTER SIX

SERVANT OF THE POOR AND SUFFERING

Have no anxiety at all, but in everything by prayer and petition,
with thanksgiving make your requests known to God.

Philippians 4:6

Martin's devotion to daily prayer and penance gave him the peace and serenity to ask our loving Savior for many gifts and graces, not for himself but for those whom he served. One of Martin's special joys came from his service of the poor.

Feeding the Poor

At the close of each day, hundreds of beggars waited at the monastery door for the one they called, "Father of the Suffering Poor." After the priests, brothers, novices, and those in the infirmary had eaten, Martin gathered the remains of the meal to distribute to the people outside.

Waiting expectantly would be widows, orphans, Indians, Africans, the sick, and even servants of Spanish nobility who had lost their money but were too proud to come themselves. Mixed in the group might be dogs and cats that roamed the streets and somehow knew that Martin would not neglect them.

No matter how large the group, the remnants of bread and soup that Martin brought were always enough to nourish all who came. Just as Jesus multiplied the loaves and fishes for the crowd who came to listen to him, he multiplied Martin's food so that it was always sufficient. After all were fed, Martin spoke to the crowd about Jesus' love for the poor and his special love for each of them. Martin's comforting words and his counsel to remain faithful to and hopeful in the Lord did as much to sustain and strengthen the crowd as the bread and soup.

Caring for the Sick

Besides feeding the poor, Martin also cared for the sick among them. If someone needed sustained attention, he would take the person to his cell. His cell was small and contained only a plank for a bed, but it was more comfortable than lying on the street.

On one occasion a brother was helping Martin change the sheets on his bed after caring for a sick person. The brother complained, "How are we ever going to clean these sheets of the blood and the drainage from infection?"

Martin was upset with the comment and answered, "A little soap and water will clean the sheets, but only penance will remove the stain of uncharitable words."

When Martin was finally asked to stop treating the sick and wounded in his cell, he went to his sister, Juana, who lived some distance away, and begged her to provide room for the sick. He then visited each day to care for them.

He also frequently visited the servants and workers at the farm at Limatambo, the Dominican retreat. More than food and often-needed medical attention, he brought the workers words of simple faith spoken with his gentle manner. He explained the necessity of belief and the importance of relying on the Savior's suffering to make up for all sin.

Visiting the Imprisoned

Martin's efforts to ease the life of the poor extended to those in prison. As usual, he brought both physical and spiritual nourishment. One day he had dispensed all the food that he had brought only to realize that two prisoners had not been fed. He left the prison to find a dealer in used clothing. Certainly, his ragged habit could not be sold, but he had worn a hat to protect his head from the heat of the sun. He sold his hat, bought food, then returned to feed the two who had been neglected.

One prisoner who was to be executed the following day was frightened of death and God's final judgment.

Martin prayed with him, saying "You will not be executed."

The next day the prisoner was led out to be hanged. He must have wondered why Martin had falsely encouraged him the night before. But just as the hangman was about to slip the rope around his neck, he received a pardon. However, his troubles were not over because he had no way to earn a living. Martin was there again to help him find employment and to give him a small sum of money to help him start a new life.

Knowing Martin's unfailing help, two men suspected of a crime rushed to his cell for assistance. The police were right behind them because they also knew that Martin's cell was a likely place of refuge. His room that day contained two large baskets of laundry. When the police knocked on his door, he fell to his knees in prayer and instructed the two fugitives to hide in the baskets and to pray as well.

The knocking continued until Martin finally opened the door. Since the baskets were the only place that the two could have hidden, the officers sifted through the baskets carefully but to no avail. The two suspects felt the officers' hands on them during the search, but they remained invisible and undetected. Overjoyed at their escape, they thanked Martin and begged his pardon for having caused the disturbance.

Helping the Common Soldier

Another group that received Martin's aid was the soldiers camped near the city. Having been brought to

the New World to subdue the Incas and protect the Spanish settlers, the soldiers were sometimes left without provisions while they waited for a new assignment. Martin trudged the road to the camp with food and supplies for as long as their need lasted. And again, he lifted their spirits with words of God's love and the hope of heavenly rewards for their faithful service to him.

Collecting Donations

As we have seen, Martin, who practiced the strictest poverty himself, never seemed to be without money when someone else had a need, such as the pardoned prisoner who needed to make a fresh start. No one has a record of the many times a coin or two made a difference in the life of one who came to Martin for help.

Well known in Lima since his days as a barber, Martin frequently walked the streets with a basket of food and a collection of herbs to treat the sick. In the monastery he had also become the almoner, the one responsible for the money the townspeople brought as alms or for Masses to be said. When funds, food, or clothing were needed for special projects, he would approach the rich of the city asking for donations. Often he was able to collect as much as $2,000 in a day, an enormous sum for an individual to collect even today. Back then, it was a staggering figure.

Where and how Martin got the funds for his various projects was sometimes a mystery. However, once he bought clothes for the ragged poor, using money his niece Catarina, Juana's daughter, had saved for her wedding garments. Just as Martin's mother had been angry when he gave away their food money as a boy, so, too, was Catarina upset. But one of Martin's benefactors heard of Catarina's loss and soon replaced the money.

Building an Orphanage

Martin's biggest challenge came when he saw the many children who roamed the city streets. He often saw these beloved of Jesus hungry, homeless, and entirely without loving care. Sometimes he brought them gifts of fruit, bread, and even shoes when he saw their need. He always spoke to them of God's love. Martin knew it was inevitable that such children would come to harm if left homeless and would probably turn to crime. An orphanage was needed.

He approached Lima's viceroy, other government leaders, and high church officials with his plan for building a home to shelter and educate the children. No one was either willing or able to finance such a project. So Martin, fired by his love of God, began alone going to the rich of the city, asking for funds to begin the project. Once several had contributed to the cause, others who had at first been unwilling or unable to help also contributed. Soon the Orphanage of Holy Cross became a reality.

But a building providing food and shelter was not enough. The boys needed an education so they could develop the skills that would help them become self-sufficient. The girls needed first an education and then a dowry of money or goods, so they could attract a good husband. Martin helped see that all needs were provided for.

Calming the Waters

Martin served the city of Lima as a whole when torrential rains swelled the Rimac River. Its out-of-control flooding had already caused serious damage along its banks and more was threatened. The people were terrified. When rising waters endangered a church dedicated to Our Lady, filled with beautiful pictures and statues that needed to be saved, someone at last thought to call Martin for help.

Martin came down to the river's edge, picked up three pebbles, and began praying to the Holy Trinity. He placed one pebble at the edge of water and called on the Father. The second stone he threw a short distance into the raging water and invoked the Son. He threw the third pebble as far into the current as he could while he called on the Holy Spirit. Then he knelt to continue his prayer. The citizens who had gathered also dropped to their knees to pray and watched as the waters slowly receded.

Amazed by the miracle, the people of Lima decided to build the church farther from the banks to avoid another flood. Martin told them their efforts were not necessary. The river would never again threaten the church. And it has not.

Traveling to the World's Needy

Martin wanted to become a missionary and to travel to distant lands to bring the word of God to all. When many of his fellow Dominicans had recently been martyred in Japan, Martin wanted to offer the sacrifice of his life to God. But this was not in God's plan. Even when the archbishop of Mexico, whom he had healed earlier, wanted Martin to go with him to Japan, Martin's superiors refused permission. They knew how valuable his work in Lima was. Still, God answered Martin's desire by giving him the very special gift of bilocation, the ability to be in more than one place at one time. This allowed him to continue his life in the monastery while also performing good deeds at a distance, sometimes a great distance. Since Martin always appeared to be wherever he was needed, perhaps he used this gift more times than are recorded.

For example, once his sister Juana and her husband were having a serious disagreement. Suddenly, Martin appeared there with them, with his gentle words and a gift of wine and fruit. He understood without being told the cause of the argument and was soon able to bring them to a peaceful understanding. The next day Juana mentioned to someone in the monastery Martin's helpful visit. The friar was amazed because he knew Martin had not left the monastery at all the previous day.

There is also the mystery of the out-of-season orange that Martin had brought to the friar who was ill. Did Martin travel someplace far away to find the orange? One of his distant travels must have taken him to

France. Once, when questioned about an unusual healing treatment he used in the infirmary, he replied without thought, "I saw it done this way in France, in the hospitals of Bayonne."

Martin was also reported to have frequently visited Christians in Algeria who were prisoners of the Muslims. The Christians were badly treated in an attempt to make them renounce their faith. Martin brought them food and money, but most importantly he brought them comfort and encouragement to remain faithful. These visits to the African continent came to light in a strange way.

A traveling Spaniard came to the monastery one day. Passing Martin in the hall, he recognized the one who had offered him support during his many years of imprisonment in Algeria. He began to thank Martin for all he had done, but Martin, always reluctant to accept thanks, rushed on saying, "I am busy just now."

The visitor was bewildered at this brusque dismissal and related to several friars the story of Martin's visits. The Spaniard explained that he had been able to purchase his release from slavery by saving the money Martin offered during his several visits to the prison. The friars knew, however, that Martin had never left the monastery for such extended travel and certainly had never left Peru for Africa.

Reflection

Sometimes people may not be pleasant, may have annoying habits, or may be poorly clothed and unwashed. These are all external things. Martin, following the example of Christ, loved and served all people to the best of his ability. And so must we serve, to *our* best ability, those who present their needs to us. We can do as Martin did and see in all those we meet the presence of Our Lord.

St. Martin de Porres, pray for us.

Thánh Martin de Porres, caú cho chúng con.

San Martín de Porres, ruega por nosotros.

CHAPTER SEVEN

MARTIN'S LOVE OF ANIMALS

All creatures great and small,…
The Lord God made them all.
From "All Things Bright and Beautiful"
Mrs. Cecil Frances Alexander

Martin's heart was so filled with love of his Creator that his love could not help but spill over and pour out on all God's creatures, even the birds and the beasts. Martin's concern for animals is not his most important work, but one that endeared him to others both during his life and after his death. Like St. Francis of Assisi before him, he recognized that animals are valuable in God's sight and that humans have a responsibility to care for and protect them. Those who had known Martin and witnessed his kindness to animals told many wonderful stories at the process for his beatification.

Martin and the Mice

One of the most famous and often-retold stories is about Martin's encounter with mice. One day the sacristan, the priest who cared for the altar and altar linens, was flushed with anger.

"What is troubling you?" Martin asked, seeing the man's red face.

"Martin, you must put down poison for the mice. They are eating holes in the altar cloths. The holes are so large, I probably won't be able to repair them," the sacristan sputtered.

"How terrible," Martin responded, "but we must not harm the poor mice. They are only hungry and are probably trying to build soft nests for their young. Let me see what I can do."

Martin then captured a mouse and, cupping the soft, quivering creature in his hands, he said, "Brother Mouse, you, your relatives, and your friends are destroying the fine linen used in our worship of Our Lord. This cannot continue."

The mouse gazed up, as if listening carefully. Martin continued, "You and all the others must move outside to the garden or the barn, and I will see that you are fed each day."

Martin released the mouse, which immediately scampered toward the garden. Soon mice scrambled from all corners of the monastery out of closets, cupboards, and holes in the wall. The swarm of mice quickly settled in the area Martin had suggested and, true to his promise, he fed them faithfully every day.

In another incident, a Dominican went to the kitchen on an errand. Before he entered, he glanced in the door and observed a dog and cat enjoying, side-by-side, the same bowl of soup. Martin, who had provided the soup, was also watching. Then he noticed a mouse hovering nearby. He said, "Come, little mouse, and share the meal. There is enough for all of you to eat together." The mouse immediately joined the dog and the cat at the bowl. These three that are often enemies ate peacefully side by side. It is no wonder that people invoke Martin when their homes are troubled by mice and rats. Prayers to Martin seem to rid the home of these visitors even without a promise to feed them.

Caring for Birds

The monastery kept chickens to supply meat and eggs. When Martin entered the chicken house, the birds flocked around him. Chickens do that, of course, when they are expecting food, but these chickens were longing just to be close to Martin. Perhaps they knew that he himself ate only bread and fruit. He would pick up the chickens, talk softly to them, and pat their feathers. They seemed to sense some of their Creator's love flowing from Martin's heart.

One day as Martin was weeding in the garden, a hawk fell at his feet. The hawk's wing had been damaged, perhaps by a hunter's shot or a stone from a boy's slingshot. Hawks can be dangerous, especially when they have been wounded, but Martin had no fear. He gently picked up the injured hawk to study the damage. The hawk rested quietly in his hand while he decided how best to treat its wing. After cleaning the wound and bandaging the torn wing, he placed the hawk on the ground.

For several days the hawk remained close to Martin until its bandage was removed. With its wing healed, the hawk soared into the sky. But it remained nearby and later, whenever Martin spent time in the garden, the hawk would circle and land at his feet as if to thank him for his care.

Caring for Dogs

Martin also showed great love for dogs. Perhaps he cared for them because so many wandered loose around the city. Moreover, St. Dominic, the founder of Martin's beloved Dominicans, is often pictured accompanied by a dog.

One of these street animals was a bully and frequently fought with other dogs. Bested in one fight, it was seriously wounded, and so it came to Martin for help. Even though the dog growled and bared his teeth, Martin cared for it. He said, however, "Once I make you well, you must cease your fighting."

When the dog was healed, Martin warned it again to behave itself. The dog remained with him as a kind of watchdog for some time. Unfortunately, it did not take Martin's advice to become gentler. After it nipped at one of the friars, it was banished from the monastery.

The people of Lima often brought their sick and wounded dogs and cats to Martin. And frequently these animals, like the bully dog, sought him out themselves. Sometimes after treating an animal, Martin would send it on its way saying, "Stop by tomorrow and let me see how you are doing." The animals obeyed, returning for more help or just as a sign of their gratitude.

Eventually, the crowd of ailing and injured creatures was too much for the priests and brothers in the monastery. Martin was told to stop bringing sick animals into his cell. Ever obedient, but still concerned, he talked to Juana. He begged his sister to take in the dogs and cats that needed care. As she had accepted the sick and suffering people who had sought Martin out, she also gladly accepted responsibility for the animals. Each day, Martin traveled the mile and a half to her home and gave whatever care was necessary to heal the dogs and cats she was sheltering.

On one of his visits, Juana complained that the dogs were becoming a nuisance, doing what dogs do and using her yard as their personal bathroom.

"Martin," she said, "you must do something. I can't tolerate any longer the mess these dogs are making."

Martin understood her concern and spoke to the dogs, which had assembled to greet him. "You will not be welcome here if you continue making a mess. You must go to the street to take care of your needs." The animals listened attentively and immediately changed their habits, so that Juana was happy to continue to shelter them.

Animals Brought Back to Life

Once day as Martin and others were walking to the country retreat of Limatambo, they met a crowd gathered at the side of the road. The roadside sloped and in the deep ravine next to it a donkey lay dead. Martin spoke to it, "Creature, arise."

To the wonder of the watching crowd, the donkey struggled to its feet and clambered up the hill. At best, donkeys are not known for their obedience, even to the words of their masters. In addition, this one had been to all appearances dead.

Later, back at the monastery, another donkey was suffering from a broken leg. One of the brothers had decided it was necessary to kill the animal. He said, "A donkey with a broken leg is of no use for work." When Martin saw the otherwise healthy donkey, he spoke to it. "Creature of God, heal." In a few days the donkey was able to return to its duties.

One of the dogs Martin cared for lived in the monastery. For 18 years it had been the companion of the priest in charge of the kitchen. But because of its age, the dog had mange, a skin disease, and also a terrible odor. The priest decided the dog should be killed and asked a servant to do it. One day as the dog was sleeping in the garden, the servant saw the opportunity to kill it, lifted a rock, and crushed the dog's head. As the servant was preparing to bury the dog, Martin approached.

He carefully lifted the dead animal into his arms and took it to his cell. There he cleaned and dressed the wound. Amazingly, the dog returned to life and in a few days was restored to health. It no longer had the mange nor was it odorous. From that time on, the dog was Martin's faithful companion. Martin gently admonished the dog's owner, "We have a responsibility to care for life that God has given."

Calves, Bulls, and Mosquitoes

In the sixteenth century people lived differently than we do today. Animals roamed freely. In addition, they not only served as work companions, they often provided sport and amusement in ways that would now be judged cruel.

Someone had brought some calves to the monastery to entertain the novices. After a few hours, the novices tired of the calves and enclosed them in a room. Going about their duties, they forgot the calves for several days. When Martin happened on the animals, they were starving. They could have crushed him in their attempt to escape and find food, but instead they milled around him, sensing that he would provide for their needs, which of course he did.

Calves may have been amusing, but bulls were frightening animals. An angry bull was to be avoided at all costs. One day the monastery was in an uproar. A bull had gotten inside and was blocking the door so that no one could enter or leave. Martin was taking a guest to the door when he encountered the bull. Instead of running for cover, he instructed his guest to wait behind him while he approached the animal.

Speaking softly, Martin said, "Brother Bull, you are causing havoc here. Return to the street where you

belong." The bull bowed its head, not to attack, but as if in shame for its behavior. It left the monastery doorway.

One summer Martin had been working outside, his back bared to the hot Lima sun. When another brother saw Martin's back covered with mosquito bites, the brother said, "The mosquitoes have made a meal of you. You should protect yourself."

"Aren't we instructed to give food to the hungry?" Martin asked.

"Yes, but isn't that rule intended for people, not mosquitoes?"

Martin's reply sums up his attitude: "Mosquitoes, too, are creatures of God and should be fed."

Reflection

Martin's love for all creatures models what human behavior should be. He realized that God made animals for our use, and consequently they deserve our care and concern. We have a responsibility to protect the environment, not just for our welfare, but also for the welfare of all creatures. We do not need to bare our backs to mosquitoes, but we do need to care for those animals we have taken into our homes for our pleasure. Martin's example should encourage us to look for more opportunities to demonstrate love for all God's creatures.

St. Martin de Porres, pray for us.
Thánh Martin de Porres, caú cho chúng con.
San Martín de Porres, ruega por nosotros.

CHAPTER EIGHT

MARTIN'S FRIENDS

Look to God that you may be radiant with joy...
Psalm 34:6

Martin found joy serving his brother Dominicans, working with the novices, caring for the sick and the poor, and even taking care of animals. But perhaps his greatest joy outside the time spent in prayer was the time spent with his special friends. Inspired by his overwhelming passion for God, Martin loved with complete and total love all those whose lives he touched. But some of his friends would later be raised to sainthood, and they must have been especially close to his heart.

Juan Vasquez—A Helping Friend

Not a saint, but one for whom Martin held special affection was Juan Vasquez, who appeared at the

monastery gate when he was just a 14-year-old boy.
How he had arrived in Lima is not clear because he had
no relatives or friends in the city. He had been sleeping
in the street and was close to starving. Martin took Juan
to his cell and allowed the boy to wash up. Giving him
clean garments, Martin told him that he could sleep in
his cell and eat regularly at the monastery until he
could find work.

On a night not long after, a fierce earthquake shook
the city. Juan was awakened to see Martin lifted above
the floor in ecstasy before his crucifix. The next morning, Juan raced to tell what he had seen to one of the
religious, who commented, "You will soon learn not to
be surprised by Brother Martin."

Martin, however, was not pleased when he heard
that Juan had reported what he'd seen and advised the
boy not to speak of such things. Apparently, Juan took
the advice to heart. Sometime later he came upon Martin again lifted in ecstasy and quickly closed and locked
the door so that no one would see or interrupt such pro-
found prayer.

No sooner had he locked the door than another religious came looking for Martin.

"He is not here," Juan said.

The boy immediately regretted the lie but had only
intended to protect his friend and benefactor. He had
more cause for regret when the brother, seeing the key
in his hand, demanded it and unlocked the door. Peer-
ing inside, the brother saw nothing. Martin was invisible and thus spared both himself and his young friend
embarrassment.

Much later, after Martin's death, Juan was still reluctant to tell of these wonders until Martin appeared to him and said that it was now acceptable for Juan to tell the things he had observed.

While Martin was still alive, he decided the young man should begin to earn his way in the world. "What trade do you know?" Martin asked.

"I have no skills that will allow me to be employed," the youth replied with shame.

"Then I will teach you the skill I learned as a youngster. You will be a barber."

Soon Juan was competent enough to cut Martin's own hair as well as the hair of the other friars, thus relieving Martin of that responsibility. By this time, the young man was devoted to Martin and became an almost constant companion.

Once when Martin and Juan were visiting Limatambo, Brother Christobel decided that a particular piece of uncultivated land was an excellent place for an olive grove. Planting the grove would take several men a few days and would be difficult work. Since the young trees were already there and ready to be planted, Martin and Juan began immediately. Martin dug holes, and Juan planted the young trees and packed the earth carefully around the roots.

In the cool darkness of evening, Brother Christobel returned to the field. He was pleased to see in the dim light that the work of planting had been started.

"Will you return tomorrow to finish?" he asked Martin.

"We have already planted all the trees," Martin said.

Brother Christobel was amazed and returned the

next day in morning light to view the grove. The young trees were indeed all planted.

Sometime later, Martin entrusted Juan with a very sensitive mission.

Many Spanish widows and orphans of formerly wealthy families were now suffering great hardship. They knew no skills, so they could not be employed and were too proud to beg. Martin wanted to see to their needs privately to avoid embarrassing them. He, perhaps, also felt that they could accept help from a Spaniard like themselves better than from a mulatto, so Juan was given the task of seeing to their needs.

Juan Macias—A Spiritual Friend

Another Juan was a dear spiritual friend of Martin's and would be raised to the rank of saint by the church. Juan Macias, who grew up in Spain, was only a few years younger than Martin. He was the orphaned son of a noble Spanish family that had lost all its money. Raised by an uncle, from age five he spent his days tending sheep. Being alone on a hillside all day, Juan used his time for fervent prayer. When he was very young, he decided to say the entire rosary, all 15 decades, every day for himself and for sinners. This was a habit he continued his whole life. His ardent devotion to Our Lady, as well as to his patron, John the Evangelist, brought him visits from these heavenly friends.

Mary's visits rewarded the orphan with a mother's comfort. Following her instructions, Juan left Spain for the New World. After long travels and many different kinds of work, the young man arrived in Lima. There he became a herdsman, just as he had been in Spain, and he wondered why he had been led on this long and perilous journey.

A few years later after continued fervent prayer, Juan realized he was being called to be a Dominican lay brother. The holy young man presented himself at another Dominican monastery in Lima, St. Mary Magdalen, and was accepted in the Order. Like Martin, his life of virtue was remarkable, fed by his prayer and the discipline of his body. And also like Martin, Juan was responsible for feeding the poor at the gates of his monastery.

Exactly how these two holy souls found one another is not recorded, but find each other they did. They grew in holiness together as they shared prayer, spiritual discussions, and penance. On their free day once a month, they would meet at one of their monasteries, find a quiet corner where they would be undisturbed, and delight in sharing their love for their mutual friend, Our Lord. They must have also shared their concerns for and devoted their prayers to the poor and suffering of Lima. Martin no doubt spoke of his dream of creating an orphanage for the children of the streets and received encouragement from the words and prayers of his spiritual brother. They both knew that, left alone on the streets, the children would never come to know of God's tremendous love for them.

When Martin would appear at the gate of St. Mary Magdalen, he greeted Juan with the customary greeting, "Praised be Jesus Christ."

Juan would respond with joy, "Forever and ever. Amen."

One day Juan was particularly happy to see Martin because a young novice was in special need of the mulatto's healing powers. Brother Louis had accidentally cut his hand several days before, and it had become seriously infected.

"I hope you can see to Brother Louis' hand," Juan said as he led Martin inside. "You know if he loses his fingers, he cannot be ordained a priest. So he is suffering now not only from physical pain, but also from this fear."

When they reached Brother Louis' room, Martin led the young man to the garden outside, encouraging him as they walked that God would heal the cut. Martin removed the bandage to find the fourth finger nearly severed and the hand dangerously infected. Louis was in terrible pain, and his arm felt paralyzed. Martin looked for a healing herb in the garden and, finding one, crushed its leaves and applied it to the wound. Making the sign of the cross over Louis, he assured the novice that he would soon be healed.

Louis was surprised. He had anticipated something more impressive from the famed healer. Nevertheless, the swelling was going down and his arm already felt better. By the next day, he was able to use his fingers and hand again. The scars, however, remained for the rest of his life as a testament to Martin's blessed healing power.

Sometimes Juan and Martin met at Limatambo for their uplifting and mutually encouraging conversations. Together they performed severe penances to beg forgiveness for their own sins and the sins of others. The black mulatto and the white Spaniard, dressed in the black and white of their Dominican habits, were united in their love of God. Juan would remain to do God's work on earth for six years after Martin's death.

Little Rose

Another Dominican, and the first to be declared a saint of the New World, is also sometimes identified with Martin. Saint Rose of Lima was baptized in the same church and at the same font as Martin, seven years later. She lived just a block from the house where he was born and was closely associated with his monastery of Santo Domingo. Tradition has long believed that the two knew each other and were friends, although new research now questions that.

Rose, a beautiful young woman, had been born into a noble Spanish family of Lima. It was the wish of her family that she marry well and enjoy the life she had been born to. This, however, was not Rose's desire. She used things such as pepper and lye to attempt to mar her face, but her inner beauty continued to shine.

Rose was a member of the Third Order of St. Dominic. This meant that she was a lay member of the Order. Although she was allowed to wear its habit, she did not have to live in community with the other members. Out of obedience to her parents, she stayed at home but built a small hermitage on her parents' property. There she spent her time in prayer, in making beautiful pieces of embroidery to sell for money for the needy, and in visiting with the poor who came to her with requests for prayers and help.

Rose's spiritual guide, Father Juan de Lorenzana, was the priest who had welcomed Martin to the monastery of Santo Domingo. In addition, Rose frequently attended Mass at the monastery. So despite the new research, it would not have been completely unlikely for Rose and Martin to have known one another.

Tradition says that when the sick asked Rose for help, she often sent them to Martin for both his special healing powers and his prayers. In addition, Martin was able to find money to provide 27 young women with dowries for their weddings. Perhaps it was Rose who had suggested they seek him out.

Rose died 22 years before Martin did. He no doubt attended the funeral of this saintly woman who even then was hailed by the people of the city as the holy Rose of Lima. She was canonized in 1671.

Other Saints of Lima

God graced the city of Lima with two other saints during Martin's lifetime, who undoubtedly were an inspiration to him as he lived his life of prayer, penance, and service. One of these was Archbishop Turibio de Mongrovejo, who arrived in Lima in 1581 and immediately began a reform of the clergy. He confirmed the young Martin. He died in 1606 after working for the conversion of the Native Americans.

Another saint of Lima was the Franciscan Francis

MARTIN DE PORRES

Solano who arrived in South America in 1589. He worked especially to convert slaves and Native Americans. It is said that in Lima 9,000 listeners were converted during a single sermon. Both he and Archbishop Turibio were canonized in 1726.

Reflection

Our choice of friends and companions has a tremendous influence on us. As we see from Martin, friends can inspire us to greater love and service of God. Juan Vasquez grew in the reflection of Martin's glory. Juan Macias and Martin certainly encouraged one another in their service of the Lord. Rose and the other holy souls of Lima offered inspiration to Martin as well as to the city. We, too, can inspire others to good actions and deeper devotion to prayer by our example. In turn, we should choose our friends carefully with regard, not to race or riches, but to how these friends reflect God's love for all.

St. Martin de Porres, pray for us.
Thánh Martin de Porres, caú cho chúng con.
San Martín de Porres, ruega por nosotros.

CHAPTER NINE

Martin's Holy Death

Remain faithful until death, and I will give you the crown of life.
Revelation 2:10

Martin had lived at Santo Domingo for 45 years. He was now 60 and was not feeling well. His constant fasting and penance had taken a toll on his body. He also suffered frequently from a malaria-type illness, but his latest attack was something more. Just as he had known when others would die, he knew that this illness would be his last. He asked for a new habit. This in itself was extraordinary. When one of the brothers asked him why, Martin answered, "This is the habit I will be buried in." He was announcing his own death.

Martin Goes to Bed

Word spread around the monastery like a brush fire gone wild. Not only was their beloved Brother Martin

85

ill with fever, but he had said he would die in four days. The prior insisted that Martin be moved from the plank in his simple cell to a more comfortable bed in the infirmary. The prior also requested a clean, soft robe to replace the sackcloth that Martin usually wore. Martin endured all this patiently for a day. Then he insisted the soft cloth was painful and asked that it be removed. He would rest better in the familiar sackcloth with the iron chain he customarily wore wound tight around his body.

The doctor was summoned and began to try to treat his high fever and extreme chills. Martin had never before received the care of a doctor. *He* had always been the one serving and caring for others. But as always, he accepted the prior's wishes. One of the remedies the doctor recommended required the killing of chickens to prepare a special medication to be applied to the patient's body. When Martin learned of this, he refused, saying, "Don't kill the poor chickens. No medicine will end this illness." Even close to death, he did not want other creatures to suffer unnecessarily on his behalf.

Offering Comfort to Others

Through these last days, Martin never lost his beautiful smile and serene look although his head throbbed with pain. When those in the monastery came to see him, he offered them words of love, peace, and comfort. Brother Antonio, who had been assigned to care for Martin, wept at the sight of him. Martin comforted him saying, "Don't weep, little brother, because perhaps I will be more useful there than here." It was not long before he would begin his great work from heaven.

Martin's dear friend, Francisco Ortiz, visited every day. And every day Martin asked him to pray that he would be ready for his coming journey and be admitted to heaven. Of course Francisco did. He was reluctant to leave Martin's side, although others encouraged him to do so and get some rest. Afraid that this might be the last time he would see Martin, Francisco leaned over to kiss him. Martin, weakened though he was, put his arm around him and pressed him to his face. Francisco smelled a heavenly odor that hovered around his friend. At death, several saints have exuded an odor not unlike the smell from a bouquet of roses. Francisco was the first to smell the *odor of sanctity,* as it's called, coming from Martin's body, but he would not be the last.

Martin begged everyone to pray for him and to forgive him for his many sins: for wasting time, for being a bad example, for not serving God to the best of his powers. He had labored and prayed day and night serving his Dominican community, feeding the poor, curing those who were ill, and founding a refuge for orphans, but still he felt he had done nothing. His humility brought tears and the assurance of prayers from all those who visited.

Outside the Monastery

News of Martin's illness spread quickly through the city of Lima, and crowds gathered outside the gates to pray for their benefactor. Gathered there were

Spaniards, Indians, Africans, government officials, church dignitaries, and members of many different religious orders. Those who had received food, those who had been healed, and those who had benefited from his kind words and counsel all waited for news of his condition.

Among the dignitaries were Feliciano de Vega, the archbishop of Mexico who had sent his personal doctor to care for Martin, and the viceroy of Lima, Count de Chinchon. The archbishop had once been cured by Martin and had wanted him to travel with him back to Mexico. At different times, both the archbishop and the viceroy had frequently received advice and counsel from Martin. He had been for them a mentor and a guide.

Heavenly and Earthly Visitors

As Martin's life drew to its holy end, he received help and consolation from heavenly visitors: Our Lady, whose rosary he wore around his neck; St. Dominic, his patron and heavenly father; and St. Vincent Ferrer, a fellow Dominican who had preceded him to heaven. Martin was especially devoted to St. Vincent because of his great missionary work that Martin had long wished to imitate. These holy visitors gave him great comfort in his last hours.

Once, while he was totally absorbed in prayer with them, novice Brother Antonio received word that the viceroy had come for a last visit. Witnessing Martin's ecstasy, Brother Antonio did not know what to do. He tried to rouse the patient, but it was impossible. Full of both fear and awe, the novice left the cell and reported that Martin could not see anyone just then because he was with other important visitors. The prior was understandably upset. One did not keep someone as important as the viceroy waiting. The viceroy, however, was content to wait. He seemed to know that Martin would not keep him waiting without good cause.

A short while later, the novice returned to say that Martin would now see him. The viceroy knelt and asked Martin to pray for him that he might rule the land well and fairly. Martin replied, "I will not forget how good you have always been to me. I will ask our heavenly father's blessings for you."

Afterward, whether from anger or curiosity, the prior asked Martin, "Why did you keep the viceroy waiting?" And Martin told him of the heavenly visitors who had come to ease his way to death.

These were not his only visitors from the spiritual world. In his last days, the devil was also there to tempt and plague him. The devil had not been successful when Martin was well. Now, he no doubt thought that Martin's physical state had weakened his spirit. Sensing the struggle, Father Francisco suggested that Martin call on St. Dominic for help.

"He is already here with St. Vincent Ferrer," Martin answered.

Finally, like his Lord before him, Martin triumphed over this adversary.

His Final Moments

The Holy Eucharist was waiting in Martin's room for the prior to administer the Last Sacraments. Martin lay in his bed, gazing at the crucifix he held in his hand. A loud clapper sounded in the monastery to call the priests, brothers, novices, and lay servants not already present to come to Martin's bedside. Some were gathered in the room, but most were outside in the hallway. According to Dominican custom they sang the beautiful hymn to Our Lady, *Salve Regina*. This prayer to Our Holy Queen pleads with Mary to lead us to Jesus after our exile on earth. The hymn must have given great comfort to Martin, whose devotion to Mary had begun when he was just a child living with his mother and sister.

After the *Salve Regina*, Martin requested that the *Credo* be chanted. This prayer of faith honors the Trinity—Father, Son, and Holy Spirit. It renewed for Martin the whole purpose of his life: to believe fervently and to serve others with the loving devotion that was a sign of his belief. At the words "and the Word was made flesh," his hands released his crucifix and his soul departed. The archbishop traced the sign of the cross on Martin's forehead and gently closed his eyes. The friars began the customary prayers for the dead. It was 9 P.M. on November 3, 1639.

Preparation for Burial

Several religious remained to prepare Martin's body for burial. They were to clothe him in the new habit he'd said would be used for his funeral. First they had to remove the sackcloth, hair shirt, and iron chain that he had worn for so long. They were amazed to see his scars and wounds, the marks of his constant penance. How could a body punished so severely have served others with such untiring devotion, they wondered?

Soon his remains were brought to the church. Many of the friars were already there and would remain through the night until the doors were opened for all who would come to see Martin for the last time. One of those friars was Father Cypriano. He went up to the *catafalque*, the raised display platform. Father Cypriano—the once fat and stupid novice, nephew of the archbishop—was overcome at the sight of Martin's stiff, cold body.

"How can this be, Martin?" he prayed. "You must ask God to make your body flexible and lifelike to strengthen the faith of the crowds that will soon be here."

Within minutes Martin's face returned to its usual expression of peaceful serenity. Father Cypriano was overjoyed. Surely this was a sign that God had answered Martin's prayer and thus that his dear friend was in heaven.

The Faithful Arrive

Early in the morning the crowds began to gather outside the church. Without television or radio, news of Martin's death had spread rapidly throughout the city. Hundreds were waiting to see the humble mulatto who had been their friend and benefactor. They were amazed at his appearance. He looked as if, at any moment, he would smile and speak to them. At the same time, the heavenly odor that his friend, Francisco Ortiz, had first smelled filled the church.

One by one the people approached for a last look, a last touch, a last moment of prayer that Martin would continue to care for them. They touched him with their rosaries and carried away small pieces torn from his habit. These became for them sacred relics of the servant of God whom they knew to be a saint. His new habit was soon so shredded it looked worse than the tattered one he'd been accustomed to wear in life. His body had to be clothed in a new habit several times before the vast procession ended. It was said that many who arrived limping or suffering other infirmities walked away healed.

Funeral Mass and Burial

It seemed that all of Lima crowded the church for the Requiem Mass.

Among those attending were the archbishop of Mexico, the bishop of Cuzco, the viceroy of Lima, and the judge of the Royal Court of Lima. At the end of the Mass, Martin's body was to be carried by four novices to the Dominican burial place beneath a special room in the monastery. But the archbishop, the viceroy, the judge, and the bishop insisted upon carrying Martin's body themselves to what was assumed to be its last resting place. Because of the holiness of his life, Martin was buried among the priests rather than with the lay brothers. At the end of the service the archbishop said, "Yes, this is the way saints should be honored," expressing the thoughts of all who had gathered.

Reflection

Martin had assured those who waited by his deathbed that he would be more help to them from heaven than he had been on earth. This assurance offers comfort to us. Whether we are trying to make decisions about some direction in our lives or are suffering mentally, physically, or emotionally, Martin is there to help us if we ask. If Martin was concerned about the welfare of mice, he is certainly concerned about us.

Everyone wants a holy death when the time comes. We may not be surrounded by heavenly or important earthly visitors, but if we have tried to live a life of love and service as Martin did, we should find a welcome in heaven.

St. Martin de Porres, pray for us.
Thánh Martin de Porres, caú cho chúng con.
San Martín de Porres, ruega por nosotros.

CHAPTER TEN

EARLY MIRACLES

The Lord God will wipe away the tears from all faces.
Isaiah 25:8

Grief at Martin's death was tempered in all by the knowledge that his great faith in his Lord and Savior had secured a place for him in heaven. Hadn't Jesus said to the thief hanging on the cross beside him, "This day you will be with me in Paradise"? All believed that Martin was looking down from one of the many mansions in heaven and would help his friends as he had promised. The beautiful odor present in the church during the funeral seemed to confirm this. And after the funeral, the archbishop had remarked, "Yes, this is the way a saint should be honored." He stated what all those gathered believed. From the moment of Martin's dying, the people of Lima revered him as a saint. This city, filled with a few rich and many poor, and tainted with greed and corruption, looked to Martin immediately for help in its difficulties.

First Miracle

Even before Martin's body had been taken to the church, he was ready to help his Dominican brothers. Father Juan de Vargas was in the infirmary and suffering such intense pain that he cried out for help. The brothers carrying Martin's body to the church stopped to see if there was anything they could do to ease his suffering. After determining that there was not, they suggested that Father Vargas invoke the help of Brother Martin. Father Vargas immediately called upon Martin, who had helped so many in the same infirmary over the years. He soon fell into a deep and restful sleep. When he awoke in the morning, he was completely cured.

Martin's Caregiver Suffers from Fever

Just two days after Martin's death, Brother Antonio, who had cared for him in his last illness, contracted the same fever. His illness was so severe that the doctors decided there was nothing they could do to help. The Blessed Sacrament was reserved on a little altar near his bed so that the Last Sacrament could be administered. Finally, Brother Antonio fell into what appeared to be a restful sleep. Suddenly, to the surprise of the brother who was sitting with him, he opened his eyes and said, "Don't worry, this time I shall not die."

"How do you know that?" his caretaker asked.

"Brother Martin, who was here, told me. He came with the Blessed Virgin, St. Dominic, and St. Catherine of Siena. They all stayed near the Blessed Sacrament,

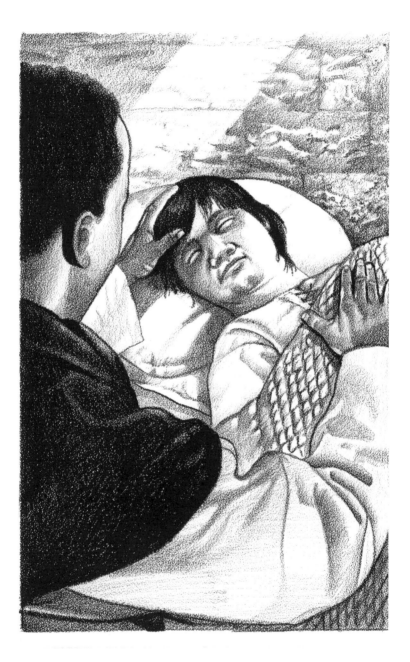

but Martin was close beside me and said, 'This visit will cure you.'"

If the other brother thought that Antonio's fever had caused him to imagine things, he changed his mind later. After a restful sleep, Brother Antonio was refreshed and ready for breakfast in the morning.

One More Favor for Father Cypriano

Father Cypriano had been protected by Martin from the teasing of his fellow novices, had been cured of serious illness by Martin, and had asked Martin after his death to appear more lifelike to inspire the faith of the public. He was now to receive still another blessing. About three years after Martin's death, Cypriano received a visitation from his departed friend.

Father Cypriano had risen high in the Order as Martin had predicted. Now he had fallen ill on his return to Lima from a trip to Rome where he had been conducting important community business. The pain in his legs felt as if he were being stuck with hundreds of needles. He reported later, "I could neither eat nor sleep and was given up by the doctors." To console him in his pain, one of his friends brought him the rosary that Martin had always worn around his neck. Father Cypriano put the rosary around his own neck and turned away from those attending him. As he did so, he saw Martin with his head bowed and his gentle smile. Martin's hands were in the sleeves of his habit, according to the Dominican custom when hands were not otherwise occupied.

Father Cypriano immediately scolded his friend. saying, "Where is your love for me, Brother Martin? You are enjoying God's presence in heaven and you have left me on earth suffering. I am not expected to live till morning."

Martin with his customary smile said, "You will not die."

Meanwhile, those watching over Father Cypriano assumed that his fever had made him delirious because he was talking to himself. They did not see the heavenly visitor. After Martin's visit, Cypriano fell into a peaceful sleep and in the morning awoke refreshed. He was soon able to resume his ordinary duties. One more time Martin had come to his assistance.

Other Cures Reported

Many others around Lima reported cures. A woman who had been crippled for 15 years was suddenly able to walk after a prayer to Martin. Another woman whom he had healed while he was alive was again ill. She asked once again for his help and was cured. Doctors had confirmed that another doctor was dying and appeared to be beyond earthly help. He appealed to Martin and was soon able to return to his duties. A six-year-old child was also dying. His eyes were closed, and he had no pulse. Frantically, his parents turned to Martin for help. As soon as the prayer was finished, the parents noted improvement. The young boy opened his eyes, and his pulse was again beating normally. Soon he was able to return to play.

Building a Special Shrine for Martin

These wonderful happenings drew many to Martin's burial place to ask for his intercession. Over the years, many devoted petitioners flocked to the *Convento* of Santo Domingo and the Church of Holy Rosary, and this created a problem. Martin had been buried in an honored place inside the cloister, which was inaccessible to lay people. The prior was concerned about the frustration this caused the faithful. He knew the solution was to build a shrine for Martin close to the monastery, but in a place where lay people were allowed. Converting the supply room of the monastery, the room from which Martin had served the sick and poor of Lima for his whole life, would be an ideal solution.

Unfortunately, there was no money available to build a proper shrine. But then the prior had an idea. He approached a wealthy friend of Martin's, Juan de Figueroa, for assistance. Not only was Juan willing to offer money for the building, but he also told the prior a remarkable story.

Several years before Martin's death, Juan had discussed with him his intention to give funds to another religious order for a chapel. By contributing to this building, Juan and his family would have the privilege of being buried there. Martin encouraged him to make this contribution but warned Juan, "You will not be buried there. You will be buried here with me." At the time, the two were standing in the supply room. Juan had not forgotten Martin's promise and was eager to contribute to the new chapel and eventually to be buried there with his holy friend.

The chapel was completed in March 1664, and plans were made to transfer Martin's body to the shrine. When his body was removed from its burial place, the sweet smell of roses that had filled the church at his funeral was evident again. Those who touched his body during the transfer carried the fragrant smell on their hands even after several washings. Not only that, Martin's body had not suffered the usual decay of death.

The transfer of Martin's mortal remains was supposed to be a secret, but somehow the word got out. Crowds gathered to visit again this holy brother who had helped them all so much. They wanted to touch his body with their rosaries, to be close to him in any way they could. Martin was soon reburied in the Chapel of the Most Holy Crucifix. He rested at the foot of the crucifix where he had spend so many hours in adoration during his life.

Another Cure

Even the earth from Martin's first burial place effected a cure. A few days after the transfer, this soil was used to cure an African, Juan Criollo, from a troublesome fever that had persisted for a long time. Doctors had prescribed a number of remedies, all to no avail. Naturally, Juan was worried that the fever would lead to his death. He mentioned his fears to Brother Lorenzo, a Dominican who had come to visit him. Brother Lorenzo had brought with him a little soil that had touched Martin's body during the second burial. To comfort Juan, Brother Lorenzo told him of the events of this last burial and of the heavenly smell that accompanied the transfer.

Then he suggested, "Take this bit of soil and mix it with water. If you drink it and ask for Martin to intercede with God on your behalf, you may be helped, if such a cure is for the good of your soul."

Juan eagerly drank the mixture and prayed earnestly to Martin for relief. In a few days, the doctor was amazed at his recovery and declared him cured.

Reflection

Martin's care and concern for those he had left behind was immediately evident. They knew his love would ever be with them, and that the favors he received from Our Lord would be many and great. A simple prayer, the touch of a rosary, even earth that had touched his body brought relief, if it was for the greater glory of God and the good of the individual. Martin's love for those in trouble, whether it be as small as passing a test or as large as the cure of a deadly disease, is still a powerful aid. Knowing all that Martin has done for others should encourage us to pray daily to him for his comfort and assistance.

St. Martin de Porres, pray for us.
Thánh Martin de Porres, caú cho chúng con.
San Martín de Porres, ruega por nosotros.

CHAPTER ELEVEN

STEPS TOWARD CANONIZATION

Blessed are the poor in spirit, for theirs is the kingdom of heaven.
Matthew 5:3

From the richest to the poorest, the people of Lima were convinced that Martin was indeed a saint, but the church had not yet placed his name among the canonized. The process of adding a saint to the church's formal list is long and complex. In Martin's time, the process was further complicated by the difficulty of communication between Lima and Rome and eventually consumed almost 300 years. In our day, rapid communication hastens the process, as will no doubt be seen in the cause of Mother Teresa. Perhaps, too, in those days, naming an African Spaniard to the list of saints was cause for procrastination.

In any case, God's time is not the world's time, but as Martin's case was delayed, devotion to him spread far beyond Lima. For example, only eight years after his death his biography was written in Spain in 1647, followed by one in Rome in 1658. But it wasn't until 1889 that the first biography in English appeared as a translation from the Italian.

The First Step

The first step toward canonization is asking the Holy Father's permission to introduce the cause. In 1659, twenty years after Martin's death, the king of Spain wrote to the Holy Father for this permission for the first time. He would send several more letters. Following his letters were similar requests from the viceroy of Lima, the archbishop of Lima, the Dominicans, and members of all the religious orders in Lima. While the letters bombarded the Holy See, the process of interviewing those who knew of Martin's work and miracles began in 1660. A notary in Lima, Francisco Blanco, was assigned to collect this information. Later, he excused himself from notarizing because he himself had turned to Martin for help. Martin effected a small healing for him that would have kept him from gathering information from a visiting archbishop. Since all this occurred about 20 years after Martin's death, many of his friends and fellow religious, as well as his sister Juana, were able to describe what they had experienced and witnessed firsthand. More than 75 depositions or testimonies were recorded and sent to Rome.

Formal Introduction of Martin's Cause

The collected evidence was sent to Rome in 1668. Papers acknowledging the cause of Martin were returned to Lima in 1678. The ship carrying the papers to Rome was lost at sea, which caused part of the ten-year delay. These papers were somehow recovered and sent on their way again. When the papers acknowledging Martin's cause were finally returned, it was a day of celebration. A huge group comprising people from all corners of Lima and from all walks of life processed from the palace of the archbishop to the Convento of Santo Domingo. An eyewitness said that it was the largest gathering of people he had ever seen in the city. Church bells were rung, and the ceremonies concluded late in the evening with fireworks and rockets.

The Apostolic Process now began in earnest. Personal statements or testimonies about the events of Martin's life were heard again. This time, more than 175 statements were recorded. Now testifying more openly was Juan Vasquez, Martin's young companion, whom he had admonished about talking to others about the wonders he had seen. Martin had appeared to Juan and encouraged him to tell this time all that he had seen. Juan willingly did. The process of collecting testimonies continued over eight years.

When these papers were sent to Rome, they were again lost at sea, but fortunately notarized copies had been made, and these were then sent. Granted that the church moves slowly, it was still some 75 years before Pope Clement XIII officially declared the heroism of Martin's virtues. This declaration made on February

27, 1763, marked Martin as one of the venerable and allowed the process to continue. Although many miracles had been attested to and more had occurred in the intervening years, two carefully documented miracles were needed before he could be elevated to the ranks of the blessed.

Two Miracles for Beatification

The first official miracle was granted Elvira Moriano of Lima. An earthen jug had slipped from her hands and shattered. As pieces of the jug flew in all directions, one struck her eye and pierced it. She lost not only her sight, but the eye as well. The pain was instant and horrible. Her cries brought her neighbors, one of whom called the best doctor in the city. Unfortunately, he said there was no hope for her sight, and he could do nothing for her. He suggested prayer as a remedy. Elvira's son was a novice at Santo Domingo, and when word of her injury reached the monastery, her son was sent to her with a relic of St. Martin. When she held the relic on her empty eye socket, the pain subsided.

Soon she fell into a restful sleep. When she awoke in the morning, she felt her wound. Surprised at what she felt, she rushed to a mirror to confirm that both her eye and her sight had been completely restored. The doctor and others attested to her cure.

The other miracle involved a little boy, Melchior Varanda, who was the two-year-old son of an African slave. His mother was cleaning the house of a wealthy Spanish lady. While his mother worked, Melchior ventured too close to a second-floor balcony railing and fell to the street some 20 feet below. The fall crushed his head and caused internal injuries. The Spanish lady immediately called a renowned doctor, who upon viewing the extent of the little boy's injuries held out no hope to the grieving mother. However, the kind Spanish lady, who had great faith in Brother Martin, brought a picture of Martin and placed it on the boy's head. Melchior appeared to be resting peacefully, and in a short time he was up and ready again for play. The doctor and many others who were present testified about this miracle.

Now again, it was time for action from Rome. More than 70 years passed before these two miracles were affirmed by the Sacred Congregation of Rites, thus clearing the way for Pope Gregory XVI to sign the decree approving the beatification of Martin, marking him as one of the blessed. In all, it had taken almost 200 years to reach this point in 1837. Martin's close friend and fellow Dominican, Juan Macias, was beatified at the same time. The two friends, one black and one white, who had encouraged one another in their earthly lives, must have rejoiced that day in a heavenly celebration.

The Long Road to Sainthood

Of course, all those who are in heaven are saints, but to be declared one by the church takes a long time, as Martin's case shows. It would be more than another hundred years (in 1962) before Martin would finally be canonized. Such delays were not unusual. For example, Juan Macias, who died six years after Martin and who was beatified with him, was not canonized until 13 years after Martin in 1975.

During all this time, Martin's ability to gain favors from Our Lord did not diminish. Large and small miracles continued around the world, and devotion to him spread. Special efforts were made by the Dominicans in the United States to introduce Martin to former African slaves, freed after the Civil War ended in 1865. A chapel built in Washington, D.C. was dedicated to him in 1866. Love of Martin also spread to Ireland, Singapore, China, India, Africa, and, of course, Spain. Recently, thousands of people from the countries of Vietnam and the Philippines have appealed to Martin for help and assistance in their lives. In all these countries, those who asked for Martin's intercession were granted favors and cures. From heaven, he was able to do the missionary work he had so longed to perform while on earth.

In 1926, Pope Pius XI, recognizing the growing devotion to Martin, allowed the final process of canonization to begin. For the 300th anniversary of his death in 1939, the president of Peru designated Blessed Martin as the patron of social justice. This needed to be officially confirmed by the church, and in 1945 Pope Pius XII issued a document declaring to the whole church that Martin was the patron of social justice in Peru.

And yet, two additional miracles were needed to move Martin's cause to sainthood. Five miracles were investigated: one that occurred in Peru in 1928; one in Detroit, Michigan, in 1941; one in 1948 in South Africa;

one in 1953 in Paraguay; and one in the Canary Islands in 1960. Only the last two were accepted for the process.

The first accepted miracle was granted to an 87-year-old woman who was dying. Doctors declared her incurable and announced she had only a few hours to live. When her daughter, Juana, living in Argentina, heard of her mother's condition, she began immediately to pray to Martin, almost without ceasing. She prayed that evening at Benediction. When she was unable to sleep that night, she said all 15 decades of the rosary asking for Martin's intercession. She hoped that if her mother couldn't be cured, she would at least live long enough for Juana to travel to Paraguay to be at her side. When Juana arrived at the hospital, she found her mother changed for the better. Those attending the woman had noticed a marked improvement at the very time Juana was praying at Benediction. More improvement had been observed while Juana was praying the rosary that night. Soon, thereafter, her mother was completely well, and she lived for seven more years.

The second accepted miracle involved a young boy, Antonio, who had been playing and accidentally dislodged a heavy cement block that fell on his leg and crushed it. At the hospital, doctors determined that the leg had to be amputated. Not only was the destruction of the boy's foot so complete that repair was judged impossible, but gangrene had begun in his toes and foot. When a friend of Antonio's mother, visiting from Spain, heard of the decision to amputate, he offered a relic and a picture of Martin. The mother rushed to the hospital and applied the relic and picture to Antonio's leg. The boy kissed the picture and he, his mother, the sisters in the hospital, as well as visitors, prayed to Martin for help. The next morning the foot was better. Several weeks later Antonio was well enough to leave the hospital. In time, his injured foot was healed well enough for him to play football. These two miracles, carefully examined and attested to by those who were present, completed the formal process. Pope John XXIII presided at a meeting of the General Congregation on March 20, 1962, when Martin's canonization was approved.

A Saint At Last

The day for the solemn celebration was scheduled for May 6, 1962. Many traveled to Rome for the great day, including Antonio who had been cured by Martin. People came from South America, Spain, Ireland, the United States, and many other countries. Peru and Bolivia sent 1,500 official representatives; Spain sent 2,000 because of Martin's Spanish heritage; the Irish numbered about 1,000; and a special group of Italian barbers came to honor their patron. Some 40,000 pilgrims gathered at St. Peter's Basilica where Pope John XXIII celebrated solemn High Mass. Just before the Gloria, the decree of canonization was read by Pope John, who said in part, "We inscribe him in the list of saints, and we establish that he be honored with devotion in the whole Church."

In his homily, Pope John described Martin's life as a model for all. He first described Martin's love for Christ in the Blessed Sacrament and in his suffering. Then the Pope continued, "Saint Martin, always obedient and inspired by his divine teacher, loved his brethren with a love that sprang from humility of spirit and unwavering faith. He loved all people because he saw them as God's children and his own brothers and sisters." Pope John concluded by again exhorting all to follow Martin's example of holiness.

Reflection

If we can learn to live peacefully with all people of all races and classes, we will be following Martin's example and furthering the kingdom of heaven on earth. Each day offers us the opportunity to reach out to others with love. We need only look for opportunities. Ask Martin's assistance to help us in bringing peace on earth by our own peaceful, prayerful words and actions.

St. Martin de Porres, pray for us.
Thánh Martin de Porres, caú cho chúng con.
San Martín de Porres, ruega por nosotros.

CHAPTER TWELVE

A LIGHT FOR THE DARKNESS

Just so, your light must shine before others,
that they may see your good deeds and
glorify your heavenly Father.
Matthew 5:16

In heaven we are told there are many mansions. We know there are many saints in these mansions, so why does St. Martin de Porres have a special message for us in the twenty-first century? Why are his good deeds a special light that can brighten today's world, bringing inspiration to us and glory to God? Looking at present-day problems through the perspective of St. Martin's life, and remembering that he is the patron of social and interracial justice, we can find many insightful answers.

Ethnic, Racial, and Religious Injustice

All over the world, perhaps even in our own neighborhoods, we see people struggling with one another over ethnic, racial, and religious differences. On a small scale—hurtful words said in class or the workplace, for example—people have been made to suffer loneliness, humiliation, even physical violence. On a larger scale, these differences have caused people to abandon their homes and be separated from their families as they flee persecution. Cities have been bombed, and lives have been lost over these differences.

Martin modeled a response to the injustices heaped upon him because of his mixed racial background. He showed us that our most important heritage is that of children of God, a heritage in which we all share equally. He saw each person as a child of God and served each the same, from the beggar on the street to the highest church or government leader. His humility and gentle spirit finally brought him not only acceptance, but also reverence from people in all walks of life. In the beginning derided as the "black dog," he was later carried to his burial place by people in the highest positions in Lima.

It is not easy to accept unjust treatment from others with a smile and a gentle response, but this reaction—especially over time—will gain more for us than angry retaliation. It is not easy to stop treating others unjustly, especially if we've rationalized it as "just a joke" or as self-defense. Instead, we must learn to see ourselves and others as Martin did—as responsible for the suffering and death of Christ and at the same time as redeemed children of God. Then we can bring peace to our families, our schools, our workplaces, and perhaps the world.

Human Rights

The issue of human rights is a continuing and far-reaching concern. It is more than the slavery still practiced in many countries. It is more than the political tortures, murders, and unexplained disappearances we may read about in newspapers. It also includes matters very close to home, such as abortion, the death penalty, euthanasia, poverty, and hunger.

St. Martin cared for all those neglected by others, even the foreign soldiers sent to suppress the native people. He fed the hungry, healed the sick, sheltered the homeless, and nourished all with encouragement and words of God's love.

How can we imitate his example? We can begin by praying for peace in our home, neighborhoods, and the entire world. Just as important is our responsibility to be "an instrument of peace," as St. Francis said. This means not arguing or fighting, helping others to mend their differences, honoring equally people of different sexual, ethnic, and racial backgrounds, and reverencing all life. These actions will honor Martin and continue to bring his special light on earth.

Materialism

Today, many of us have more of the world's goods than may be beneficial for our spiritual well-being, while others have much less even than what they truly need for survival. We have Christ's admonition that it will be easier for a camel to pass through the eye of a needle than for a rich man to enter heaven. In spite of this warning, many pile up material treasures.

One of St. Martin's most distinctive traits was his devotion to poverty. He insisted upon wearing the most threadbare habit in the monastery, even when it wasn't necessary. He ate very little, usually only bread and water. He kept no money for himself, even though he sometimes collected for the needy as much as $2,000 a day from wealthy benefactors, an incredible sum at that time.

Martin lived in a monastery, while we are still "part of this world," so many of his extraordinary acts are impossible for us. So what can *we* do? We can begin by trying to use all that is ours with awareness and gratitude. This includes not using material goods wastefully. For example, we can eat all the food we take on our plates and take only as much as we'll eat. We can take better care of our clothing and other possessions, and when we no longer use something, we can give it to someone who can. We can also begin to distinguish between our desires and our real needs. Do we really *need* the shirt with the designer logo, or do we just want it? Wouldn't a less expensive one do? The money we save might be used to provide for another's needs. We spend a lot of time getting and spending money. Is this always the best way to use our time? Could Martin's example serve to direct us to living with less so that others might have a little more of life's necessities?

With St. Martin as a guide and model, we can attempt to look upon our worldly goods as gifts from God, not as gifts for us to hoard, but gifts that allow us the grace-filled opportunity to give in turn so that all may benefit.

The Environment

The destruction of our natural environment and lack of concern for endangered species are problems today. As world population grows, peaceful adaptations must be found to preserve the earth for both humans and animals. Often, little regard is paid to the loss of a species for unimportant reasons. For example, many fur-bearing animals are endangered simply to make unnecessary garments for human adornment.

St. Martin had regard for all of God's creatures. His care for humans was neverending. It extended to people he never saw, as he planted olive and fruit trees to provide food for the poor and for hungry travelers. He loved all animals as well, even protected the mice in the monastery from being poisoned. He would not even swat the mosquitoes that feasted on his sunburned back.

We cannot heal or talk to animals as Martin did, but we can care for those that are a part of our family. And once we have taken responsibility for them, we must continue to care for them, even after the thrill of a new pet is over, or when it becomes sick or old.

We must take responsibility for our world as well. We can keep our water from being polluted by disposing of cans, paper, and other debris in a trash can. Many creatures of the sea, from manatees to turtles to fish, are damaged by waste materials thrown or flushed into our rivers, lakes, and oceans. Recycling plastic, paper, glass, and other materials is an easy way to preserve our environment. Collecting and recycling materials for a sick or elderly person who cannot do it is another way to serve.

And More

These concerns are world issues and are well-suited to be brought before the patron of social justice. But Martin also has a special message, a special light for us as individuals. His obedience, patience, charity, humility, fervor in prayer, and gentleness are each worthy of our imitation. Practicing just one of these virtues in our own lives can have a healing, transforming power and can open our hearts to a closer friendship with Our Lord.

Reflection

With prayerful study of the life of St. Martin de Porres, we should be able to find new ways to bring light to the world around us. As we look through Martin's eyes, we will find many ways to help others and to make our lives conform to the model that *he* followed: Our Lord. Maybe our contributions and actions will seem slight and insignificant, but if our actions are performed with love, they will furnish our own small mansion in heaven. Let us ask Martin for his help.

St. Martin de Porres, pray for us.
Thánh Martin de Porres, caú cho chúng con.
San Martín de Porres, ruega por nosotros.

BIBLIOGRAPHY

Cassidy, James Francis. *St. Martin de Porres: Man of Many Marvels*, Dublin: Glenmore & Reynolds, LTD, 1964.

Cavallini, Giuliana. *St. Martin de Porres: Apostle of Charity*, Trans. Caroline Howard, Rockford, Ill.: TAN Books and Publishers Inc., 1979.

Dobyns, Henry E., and Paul L. Doughty. *Peru: A Cultural History*, New York: Oxford University Press, 1976.

Filteau, Jerry. "Black Clergy Mark 500th Anniversary of Slavery in America," in *The Florida Catholic*, Jan. 18, 2001.

Garcia-Rivera, Alex. *St. Martin de Porres: The "Little Stories" and the Semiotics of Culture*, Maryknoll, N.Y.: Orbis Books, 1995.

Haywood, Ernest. *Martin: the Legend and Miracles of St. Martin de Porres*, Detroit: The Haywood Foundation, 1991.

John XXIII. "Homily Given at the Canonization of Saint Martin de Porres," www.Catholic-forum.com/saints/saintmo2.htm. (4/19/2000).

The Life of Blessed Martin de Porres (a Negro Saint) of the Third Order of St. Dominic in the Province of St. John

Baptist of Peru. Trans. Lady Herbert, New York: The Catholic Publishing Society Co., 1889.

Lovasik, Lawrence G., SVD. *St. Martin de Porres,* New York: Catholic Book Publishing, 1983.

Schultz, Fr. Bruce B., O.P. "The Life of the 'Other' Martin—Saint Martin de Porras, the Afri-Peruvian Patron of Justice," in *Black Pages,* USA INC, 1997.

———. "Retrieving the African Roots of San Martin de Porras," Unpublished Master's Thesis at Xavier University, New Orleans, 1996.

Windeatt, Mary Fabian. *St. Martin De Porres: The Story of the Little Doctor of Lima, Peru,* Rockford, Ill.: TAN Books and Publishers, Inc., 1993.